PENTEC

IN SEARCH OF HOLINESS

**25TH ANNIVERSARY EDITION
REVISED AND UPDATED**

PENTECOSTAL THEOLOGY
VOLUME 3

IN SEARCH OF HOLINESS

25TH ANNIVERSARY EDITION
REVISED AND UPDATED

David K. Bernard
Loretta A. Bernard

WORD AFLAME PRESS

In Search of Holiness

by David K. Bernard and Loretta A. Bernard

Printed in the United States of America.

Published by

Library of Congress Cataloging-in-Publication Data

Bernard, Loretta A.
In search of holiness.
(Series in Pentecostal theology ; vol. 3)
Includes indexes.
1. Christian life—Pentecostal authors.
2. Holiness. I. Bernard, David K., 1956–
II. Title. III. Series: Bernard, David K., 1956–
Series in Pentecostal theology ; v. 3.
BV4501.2.B416 1988 248.4'8994 88-10767
ISBN 0-912315-40-7

Contents

Preface to the First Edition

This book grew out of a one-semester course in Practical Holiness taught at the United Pentecostal Bible College in Seoul, Korea, and out of experiences in North America and Asia. We feel a need for a straightforward, practical book on holiness designed for all Bible-believing people. We hope that this book meets that need. We do not offer it in a spirit of legalism, or with the purpose of setting denominational and church rules. Neither do we intend it to be condemnatory or directed against any individual. We have tried to set forth the basic biblical teachings on holiness and explain how they apply to the day in which we live. The book is a statement of what we as Jesus Name, Spirit-filled Christians believe, and why we believe it.

There are probably some topics about which there are differences of opinion. We present our convictions and beliefs with the hope that they will provoke prayerful consideration and Bible study. For this reason we have tried to support everything with Bible references. We do not want readers to accept everything as dogma but to study this topic for themselves. We hope that believers will discover reasons for church teachings and will develop personal convictions. We hope that ministers will become aware of certain areas of holiness in which they must be particularly careful. We also hope to provide ministers with material they can use for teaching in the local church.

We sought to cover the subject so that the book would not be limited to one culture but would be relevant worldwide. The chapters are written to be relatively independent of each other, so that users can consult them separately. Therefore, cross references are provided when necessary. Of course, the different aspects of holiness are so interrelated that the most benefit will be gained by reading the book as a whole.

We thank Elton D. Bernard, husband and father, for suggesting, organizing, motivating, editing, promoting, and, in short, making this book a reality.

Writing this book has encouraged us to think about our lives and examine ourselves closely in many areas. Our prayer is that the book will influence others, as together we grow in grace "unto a perfect man, unto the measure of the stature of the fulness of Christ" (Ephesians 4:13).

Preface to the Second Edition

by David K. Bernard

When *In Search of Holiness* was first published in 1981, there was no other book-length treatment of this subject by Oneness Pentecostals. In the course of teaching at the Bible college in Korea, my mother developed the original notes. My father saw the need for a book on holiness and urged me to make these notes into a book.

I tackled the project in 1979 and 1980 while a student at the University of Texas School of Law. I supplemented the notes in various areas, provided documentation, and expanded the material into a book.

My father made minor editorial changes, retyped the manuscript, and submitted it for publication. It was not accepted for publication at that time, however. Therefore, he raised the money to pay for its publication in 1981 and, while traveling in the United States and Canada to raise money for missions, began selling the book. In the meantime, I marketed it to bookstores, Bible colleges, and local churches. The first two printings sold within a few months, and the Pentecostal Publishing House agreed to pick up the book for the third printing.

The book has since been translated into Bulgarian, Chinese, German, Korean, Mizo, Portugese, Russian, Spanish, and Thai; and by 2005, a total of 70,000 copies had been printed. In 1985, I wrote a sequel, *Practical Holiness: A Second Look*, to provide more discussion of the theology of holiness and of particular subjects. By 2005, 25,000 copies had been printed. In 1989 I wrote *Essentials of Holiness* as a brief treatment of the subject. This booklet has been translated into Arabic, Armenian, Bulgarian, Dutch, French, German, Hungarian, Portugese, Romanian, Russian, and Slovak, and by 2005, 40,000 copies had been printed. Clearly, there is a desire for teaching on the subject of holiness.

Because *In Search of Holiness* was originally self-published, it was never fully edited. And because it was my first book, it definitely needed editing. Therefore, with my mother's consent, on the twenty-fifth anniversary of the original publication I have prepared this revised edition. I streamlined the language, updated the discussion, and inserted current references. I rewrote every chapter to improve the manner of expression and to address contemporary issues. The basic message, content, and position remain the same. I hope it continues to be a blessing.

CHAPTER

1

Holiness: An Introduction

Follow peace with all men, and holiness, without which no man shall see the Lord (Hebrews 12:14).

Holiness defined. Holiness is one of God's basic characteristics. In reference to Him, the word denotes absolute perfection and purity. Only God is holy in Himself. When the word is applied to persons or objects, it refers to what has been separated or set apart unto God. For the Old Testament Hebrews, holiness included both the negative concept of "separation" and the positive concept of "dedication." For born-again Christians it specifically means separation from sin and the world and dedication to God and His will. Since we have received the Holy Spirit of God, we have received power over sin, disease, and the devil (Mark 16:15-18). This power over sin enables us to become witnesses that we have indeed been born again (Acts 1:8). We are able to say, "God has saved me from sin. He has brought me out of a life of sin."

We must pursue holiness in order to see the Lord. This statement, found in Hebrews 12:14, is as true as John 3:3, which says, "Except a man be born again, he cannot see the kingdom of God." After the new birth, a conflict arises between the old lifestyle (the way of the flesh) and the new (the way of the Spirit). This battle is a battle for holiness, and by God's grace we can and must win it.

The need for separation. God is holy and commands His people to be like Him (I Peter 1:15-16). Beginning with the sin of Adam and Eve, sin has separated humans from a holy God. By paying the penalty for our sins, Christ has restored the broken fellowship; but if we are to have communion with God, we must separate ourselves from the old life of sin. The choice is either separation from God or separation from sin. There are only two families—the family of God and the family of Satan, who is the god of this world system (I John 3:10; II Corinthians 4:4). There is no neutral ground. These two families are distinct and separate. One is a holy family—a holy priesthood (I Peter 2:9). The other is an unholy family. The call for separation from this unholy world is clear and explicit. "Come out from among them, and be ye separate, saith the Lord" (II Corinthians 6:17).

A living sacrifice. "Present your bodies a living sacrifice, holy, acceptable unto God, which is your reasonable service. And be not conformed to this world: but be ye transformed by the renewing of your mind" (Romans 12:1-2). Holiness includes a sacrifice of our desires and our will. We must present ourselves in a manner that is acceptable to God. It is our reasonable duty to do so. We should act in a way that is acceptable to God, regardless of the sacrifice.

Holiness is imparted by the Holy Spirit. We can only be holy by God's grace. Sanctification, or separation from sin, begins with the hearing of the gospel and continues through faith, repentance, and water baptism in Jesus' name; but it is accomplished primarily by the indwelling of the Holy Spirit (I Peter 1:2). Under the new covenant, God does not write His laws on tables of stone. But God always has laws; even in the Garden of Eden He had a law. Today God writes His laws on our hearts through faith by the Holy Spirit (Jeremiah 31:33; Hebrews 10:15-17). The Holy Spirit imparts holiness to us, transforming us from the inside out.

Holiness is taught by the Bible. The Bible does not give specific answers to the countless situations that may face an individual. That is the purpose of the indwelling Holy Spirit and the ministry. The Bible does give basic guidelines that apply to men and women of all cultures, times, and situations. The Bible tells us what God likes and what He dislikes. It teaches us about the practices and attitudes that God accepts and those He expects of His people.

Holiness is taught by Spirit-filled pastors and teachers. God has given the church pastors and teachers for the perfecting, or equipping, of the saints so that the church can grow to maturity (Ephesians 4:11-15). Pastors and teachers proclaim and explain God's message so that believers can understand and obey scriptural teaching.

Holiness is taught directly by the Spirit within

us. Jesus said, "But the Comforter, which is the Holy Ghost, whom the Father will send in my name, he shall teach you all things, and bring all things to your remembrance, whatsoever I have said unto you" (John 14:26). "But the anointing which ye have received of him abideth in you, and ye need not that any man teach you" (I John 2:27). These verses do not mean that pastors and teachers are unnecessary, but they speak of the basic attitude of holiness that abides in all who have received the Spirit. The Holy Spirit informs our conscience and leads us by impressions and convictions. The Bible is our authority for Christian living, and the indwelling Spirit helps us to make correct decisions in particular situations.

Holiness is an individual matter. "Work out your own salvation with fear and trembling" (Philippians 2:12). We cannot make our own rules for being saved, nor can we save ourselves. However, with reverence and respect we must allow God to work in our lives, being careful not to destroy what God is doing. In other words, it is ultimately each individual's responsibility to submit to the ongoing process of salvation. After experiencing the new birth, each person must endure to the end of the race. We must retain what God has given to us (Hebrews 3:14).

Personal convictions. Since each person is individually responsible to God, we must have our own convictions. We cannot rely on the convictions or lack of convictions of others, but we must seek to understand God's Word for ourselves. Of course, a definite teaching of Scripture is enough to give us a conviction. We cannot avoid obeying something in the Word of God on the ground that we do not feel a personal conviction regarding the matter.

While all Christians should obey scriptural teaching, some Christians may have certain personal convictions that others do not share. Perhaps they feel strongly that they should make a certain consecration because of their background, their vulnerability in a certain area, or their desire for a closer relationship with God. In these situations, they should be true to their convictions as long as these ideas do not contradict Scripture. "Let every man be fully persuaded in his own mind. . . . For whatsoever is not of faith is sin" (Romans 14:5, 23). At the same time, they should not try to force their personal convictions upon others. Likewise, others should respect their convictions and not belittle these ideas (Romans 14:2-6).

Holiness cannot be legislated. Holiness must be motivated by the Holy Spirit that dwells within us. Pastors have the spiritual authority and responsibility to proclaim scriptural teachings. We should follow the godly teaching and example of our spiritual leaders, for they must give a report to God concerning those He has placed in their care (Hebrews 13:17). Leaders cannot force a person to be holy, however. Holiness must be formed in the heart. This process takes place through the teaching of the Word of God and the work of the Holy Spirit. Therefore, instead of comparing denominations and churches in order to decide what to obey, we need to heed the Word of God, the Spirit of God, and godly admonition from spiritual leaders.

Holiness is maintained by love for God. Jesus said, "If a man love me, he will keep my words" (John 14:23). (See also John 14:15; I John 2:3.) God's Word warns us, "Love not the world, neither the things that are in the world. If any man love the world, the love of the Father is not in him" (I John 2:15). We will live a holy life only if we love God and do not love the world system, which is influenced by Satan. Law or fear may cause us to avoid sin to a degree, but only love will create a desire in us to avoid everything that is not like God and everything that is not conducive to His presence in our lives. When we really love someone, we seek to please that person regardless of our own preferences and conveniences. Likewise, when we truly love God, our Father and Savior, we will want to obey His Word. When we read His letters to us, we want to live according to them because we love Him.

Moreover, His Spirit enables us to be obedient. Even though our flesh may not want to obey, God's Spirit enables us to be joyful in our obedience.

Principles of holiness. The Bible teaches us how to live a holy life. Among other things, it tells us, "Be not conformed to this world" (Romans 12:2). "Abstain from all appearance of evil" (I Thessalonians 5:22). Be "temperate in all things" (I Corinthians 9:25). The underlying purpose of any specific guideline is to help us abide by these basic principles.

First, we must not imitate the world of sin. We must avoid things that represent evil. The question should not be, "How closely can we resemble the world and still get by?" or "What is the least we can do and still please God?" Rather, we should ask, "How can we draw as close to God as possible? How can we live so that we are clearly identified with Jesus Christ?"

Second, we should exercise self-control and restraint. Our flesh must always be in subjection to the Spirit. We should act in moderation and not in excess. We must not go to one extreme of laxity, compromise, and worldliness or to the other extreme of self-righteousness, hypocrisy, and religious ostentation. The principles of nonconformity to the world and temperance in all things are keys to understanding all aspects of holiness.

The Christian's attitude toward sin. As Christians, we are no longer sinners by lifestyle. We have been born again, and we have power over sin (Acts 1:8; Romans 8:4). We are part of the family of God and have taken on the personality of Jesus Christ (Romans 8:29). We are Christ's disciples, and we live according to His teachings. If we are truly Christians, that is, Christ-like, then we cannot live as sinners at the same time. In fact, we must hate sin. "Ye that love the LORD, hate evil" (Psalm 97:10). "The fear of the LORD is to hate evil" (Proverbs 8:13).

As human beings, we have different personalities. Some people are naturally more aggressive, outspoken, or outgoing, while others are more reserved or easygoing. Despite these differences, if we let the Lord rule our lives, all of us will hate sin.

The preacher's attitude toward sin. All godly preachers, regardless of their different personalities, will preach forcefully against sin and for righteousness. They have this responsibility (Ezekiel 3:17-19). They help people to understand sin and righteousness by clear teaching on these subjects. They help the church to implement these teachings by giving practical guidance. While they should welcome visitors from all backgrounds and walks of life, they have a responsibility to train believers in the practice of godliness, especially those who aspire to leadership and public ministry.

Regardless of their personal inclinations, the Holy

Spirit within preachers will anoint them to cry out against sin and cry out for holiness. The Spirit will give them boldness to rebuke, exhort, and encourage as needed. God must rule in their lives so that they will minister effectively in the power of the Spirit. At the same time, preachers who are quick to rebuke, show anger, or become intolerant will also be transformed by the Holy Spirit. They will be kind and gentle in their admonitions and will preach with compassion. When preachers are filled to overflowing with the Holy Spirit, they will preach boldly against sin but will also manifest the genuine love of God for sinners.

Some ministers are so easygoing and reluctant to hurt feelings that they cannot bring themselves to preach against sin in a specific way. Some say, "My personality does not allow me to preach against sin. I can only preach love." However, if we really love people, we cannot help but stand against sin, because sin destroys people's lives and causes them to be lost for eternity. True love means more than gentleness. If we really love people, then we will love them enough to tell them the truth even if they reject us, for truth is the only basis of salvation. We should present truth in a loving manner, but we cannot compromise truth in a misguided attempt to show love. Instead, we must speak the truth in love (Ephesians 4:15). A minister who does any less is unfit as a messenger for Christ.

True ministers do not preach merely what people like to hear. They are not to be ear ticklers or jokesters. Certainly, humor and imagination are permitted in the pulpit, but the minister's basic calling is to tell people what God wants them to hear, not what they want to hear. (See II Timothy 4:2-4.)

Preachers are messengers, not the author. Preachers cannot assume the job of the Great Shepherd. They cannot change the Word of God to please people. They are merely messengers. It is illegal for a mail carrier to change the contents of a letter. Moreover, the recipient of a letter has no right to rebuke the mail carrier for its contents or to ask the mail carrier to change it. The mail carrier is not the author and does not have authority to alter the message. Similarly, preachers merely deliver God's message to the people. They dare not change the Word of God.

Verses for victorious Christians to understand. Several verses of Scripture are important for Christians to understand with regard to sin and holiness. (See Romans 6-8 for an extended discussion of Christian living, and see the commentary on this passage in *The Message of Romans* by David K. Bernard.)

"The law of sin" (Romans 7:23). There is a law of sin that is greater than the law of Moses and greater than the law of the mind. That is, neither the Old Testament law nor human reasoning can impart power to overcome the basic sinful nature that humans have. The Bible sometimes alludes to this law of sin by the terms "old man" and "flesh."

"The law of the Spirit" (Romans 8:2). The law of the Holy Spirit is the only law that is greater than the law of sin. It is the only law that can set people free from the power of sin, because by the infilling of the Spirit we receive a new identity. When we follow the Spirit, we do not desire to sin, but the laws and desires of God are implanted in us. It is important to realize that good works cannot replace or supersede the law of the Spirit.

"Whosoever is born of God doth not commit sin" (I John 3:9). This verse simply means that the children of God do not practice sin. They do not want to sin, because they have received a new identity. "For his seed remaineth in him: and he cannot sin, because he is born of God." Just like God, our heavenly Father, Christians hate sin and cannot tolerate it in their lives. However, I John 3:9 does not mean that Christians lack the capacity or ability to sin, for then it would contradict the teachings of I John 1:8 and 2:1.

As an analogy, if a certain food makes me sick, I might say, "I am sorry, but I cannot eat this food." If a certain action is not in my best interests or goes against my principles, I might say, "I cannot do this." In both cases, the word *cannot* does not mean that I am physically incapable of performing the action but that I am restrained by my nature or my knowledge. Similarly, Christians are restrained from sinning by their new identity. As long as the Spirit is in control of them, Christians will not sin. The Holy Spirit gives power over sin, and the Word of God teaches us about this power. "The word of God abideth in you, and ye have overcome the wicked one" (I John 2:14).

"Dead to sin" (Romans 6:2). "How shall we, that are dead to sin, live any longer therein?" The next few verses explain that the old man has been crucified with Christ (which takes place through repentance), so that we should not serve sin any longer. "For he that is dead is freed from sin" (Romans 6:7). Christians must understand that they are dead to sin and have been delivered from sin. As an illustration, what emotions does a dead person have? What reaction would a dead person have if we slapped him or her, or waved a million dollars in front of him or her? There would be no reaction, of course, because the person is dead. Similarly, if we are dead to sin, any temptations to sin should bring no reaction from us. If we are really dead to sin and committed to God, then living a holy life is normal. When we are half dead and half alive, however, it is difficult and eventually impossible to live for God.

Separation from God (Romans 8:38-39). Absolutely nothing can separate us from the love of God. Demons, angels, humans, trials, tribulations, time, or circumstances do not have the power to separate us from God. No one can take us out of the Father's hand, not even Satan himself (John 10:29; I John 5:18). However, Christians themselves can break their close relationship with God by unbelief and disobedience, and they can backslide. (See Romans 11:20-22; II Peter 2:20-22.)

"If we say that we have no sin, we deceive ourselves" (I John 1:8). This verse speaks of the nature of sin resident in every human being. Even though we have been born again, we still war with the flesh, or the old nature of sin. We have not yet been translated, but we await the redemption of the body (Romans 8:23). Thus, we still have the desires of the flesh and the ability to sin. Those who believe that the sinful nature has been eradicated at a certain point in their Christian experience are only deceiving themselves. While believers can and should have victory over sin and separate themselves from the desires of the sinful nature, that nature is still present within them. For this reason, it is important to maintain an attitude of being "dead to sin."

When believers receive the Holy Spirit they receive a new identity with an ability to overcome the compulsion to sin. We are called to be saints—separated, holy ones—and by God's grace we can fulfill this calling. It would be a contradiction to think of saints as sinning habitually or continuing to live a sinful lifestyle.

To illustrate, Christians have power over the sinful nature much as they do over a radio. If an unsuitable song or talk show comes over the radio, Christians can simply turn it off. They have power to prevent the radio from dominating their thoughts. Similarly, Christians have power over sin. If the Holy Spirit rules in their lives, they can "turn off" temptations when they come, preventing them from dominating their lives. When Christians sin, it is because they do not give the Holy Spirit full control at that time. They yield to a foreign master and become that master's servant (Romans 6:16).

In short, the goal for Christians is not to sin but to live a holy life. We cannot settle for being a ninety-percent Christian or a sinning Christian. "He that committeth sin is of the devil" (I John 3:8).

Do Christians remain sinners? We still struggle with the flesh, or sinful nature, but in the light of the foregoing verses of Scripture, we are not to sin habitually or to live in a sinful state. We can have ongoing victory over sin by the power of the Spirit. (See Galatians 5:16-18, 25.) As Christians, we are no longer sinners by lifestyle. We were sinners in the past, but we have been delivered and are now the children of God.

What is the position of Christians who commit sin? They have allowed themselves to fall under the influence of Satan and the sinful nature. They should immediately confess their sins to Jesus Christ, who is our advocate, counselor, and high priest. When we confess our sins directly to Him, He will forgive us. (See Hebrews 4:14; I John 1:9; 2:1.)

Personal prayer. Since confession to Jesus is the way to obtain forgiveness for sin, personal prayer is important. We should not wait until we come to church to confess our sins, but we need to confess any sin immediately and ask for forgiveness. Personal, private prayer is our communication with God. All of us need to examine our hearts and ask God to cleanse us from secret sins and faults. (See Psalm 139:23-24; I Corinthians 11:28, 31.) We need to ask for the teaching and leading of the Spirit. These prayers do not have to be voiced publicly, for this is a matter between the individual and God. Prayer is also our means of receiving power to overcome temptation and sin.

Filthiness of the flesh and spirit. "Let us cleanse ourselves from all filthiness of the flesh and spirit, perfecting holiness in the fear of God" (II Corinthians 7:1). Here, "flesh" refers to the physical component of human life while "spirit" refers to the spiritual component. This verse exhorts us to cleanse the inside and the outside, our thoughts and our actions. For instance, adultery is a sin of the flesh, but lust is equivalent to the sin of adultery in the heart (Matthew 5:28). Murder is a sin of the flesh, but hatred is its spiritual equivalent (I John 3:15). In short, we must cleanse both flesh and spirit to be holy in the sight of God.

Satan's message. The devil tries to convince us that we cannot be holy. He wants us to believe that we cannot help but sin every day. The truth is that God has commanded us to be holy. It is true that our flesh is weak, but it is also true that in the flesh Jesus condemned sin (Romans 8:3). Christ put on flesh so that through death He could destroy the one who had power over death, namely Satan (Hebrews 2:14). Jesus overcame sin in the flesh, and He is our example. We, too, can overcome sin in the flesh because we have the Spirit of Christ within us.

Perfection. The Bible teaches us that we can grow into perfection or maturity. Hebrews 6:1 says, "Let us go on unto perfection," and Philippians 3:15 speaks of "as many as be perfect." Ephesians 4:12 teaches that God gave the fivefold ministry "for the perfecting of the saints."

It is possible to distinguish between absolute perfection and relative perfection. We are all striving for absolute perfection as exemplified in Jesus Christ. Even while undergoing this growth process in order to achieve perfection, we may still be considered perfect in a relative sense if we are growing properly.

For example, a month-old child may be a perfect child even though it does not have teeth, cannot reason fully, cannot walk, and cannot talk. The child is perfect in a relative sense, because it is developing at the proper rate in relation to its age. In ten years, if this child still cannot walk or talk then it cannot be called a perfect human being. An apple bud in spring is not an apple, but that does not mean it is imperfect. Later the blossom will develop into a tiny ball, and finally it will ripen. At each stage it is perfect.

Similarly, we can obey the exhortation to be perfect by continuing to learn and grow. We must not stay in the same position as when we first came to the Lord, but we must grow in grace and knowledge (II Peter 3:18).

Tolerance because of different levels of perfection. Some people are able to develop more rapidly than others. When people of a Christian background are born again, they typically begin with a good foundation and are able to grow rapidly. Others who come from a pagan or atheistic background usually must radically change their ideas and concepts. Thus, two people may attain different levels of growth even though both came to the Lord at the same time. We are not to judge them (Matthew 7:1). In particular, fellow believers should be careful not to rebuke one another if they seemingly fail to measure up to certain teachings of holiness. It is primarily the role of the Holy Spirit and the pastor to patiently superintend the perfecting of new saints.

Not only will believers have different degrees of perfection, but so will churches. This depends on their background, foundation, and pastoral teaching. Some pastors do not teach effectively on matters of holiness, and as a result, their flock does not grow into perfection. Others build the church on the Word of God, not their own personalities, and their members can more easily grow into perfection.

"Let us go on unto perfection" (Hebrews 6:1). Holiness is a commandment for Christians to obey daily. "Be ye holy; for I am holy" (I Peter 1:16). Since God has commanded us to be holy, He will give us the ability to do so; for He does not require of us something we cannot do. Holiness and righteousness come from God. Once we are born again, God expects us to live a holy life. If we sin, we must immediately confess our sin to the Lord and receive cleansing by His blood (I John 1:9; 2:1). The

Lord wants His church to be without spot, wrinkle, or blemish—holy in His sight (Ephesians 5:27).

God's Spirit gives us the ability to live a separated life. It is our responsibility to let the Holy Spirit reign in our lives and to subdue the old nature so that we are dead to sin and the world.

As believers, we are justified—counted as righteous in the sight of God. We are also sanctified—set apart unto holiness. "But ye are washed, but ye are sanctified, but ye are justified in the name of the Lord Jesus, and by the Spirit of our God" (I Corinthians 6:11). Therefore, we can live a holy life. Instead of merely being born again and trying to rest upon that experience, let us build on that foundation. Let us be continually filled with the Spirit and grow in God's grace. Let us go on to perfection!

CHAPTER

2

The Christian Life

The just shall live by faith (Galatians 3:11).

But the fruit of the Spirit is love, joy, peace, longsuffering, gentleness, goodness, faith, meekness, temperance (Galatians 5:22-23).

Basic concepts of Christian living. When Christians talk about holiness, it is easy to emphasize rules, regulations, do's and don'ts. In a book of this kind it is difficult to be specific, plain, and honest without running the risk of seeming legalistic. This chapter attempts to put things in proper perspective by describing the basic nature of the Christian walk. The Christian life is a one of faith and liberty, not one of legalism or drudgery. Instead of merely trying not to do wrong, we are trying to bear fruit pleasing to God. Simply put, we want to imitate Christ. This chapter will define the essence of the Christian experience. Subsequent chapters will analyze what we believe to be important problem areas in today's world, but we are predicating the whole book on the concepts presented here; namely, that we live by faith not works, that the Christian experience is one of personal freedom from sin and the law, that it is a life of personal consecration to God, and that we display holiness by imitating the life of Christ and by bearing the fruit of the Spirit.

The purpose for holiness in our lives. The first reason for holiness is to please God, for His sake. He purchased us with His own blood, and we belong not to ourselves but to Him (I Corinthians 6:19-20; I Peter 1:18-19). Therefore, we cannot live to ourselves, but we must live unto Christ (II Corinthians 5:15). The second reason for holiness is to communicate Christ to others. We attract and win others to Him by the example of our lives. The third reason for holiness is for our own benefit. The Christian life of holiness is the best plan for our lives. It will benefit us both now and in the life to come.

Faith and works. We are saved by faith and not by works (Galatians 2:16; Ephesians 2:8-9). Faith leads us to repentance. True faith will cause us to obey the Word of God. It will lead us to water baptism and to the Holy Spirit baptism (Mark 16:16-17; John 7:38-39). The proper motivation for holiness is faith in God. We obey God because we trust Him. We obey His Word because we believe that it is true and that it is good for us. We do not follow holiness in order to earn salvation or favor with God, for we cannot make ourselves holy or save ourselves. Our salvation depends totally on our relationship with Jesus Christ.

Although we are not saved by our works, faith will lead us to obey what we believe. It will cause an outward manifestation, for "faith, if it hath not works, is dead, being alone" (James 2:17). We demonstrate faith in God and His Word by our actions and by our daily lives. "Shew me thy faith without thy works, and I will shew thee my faith by my works" (James 2:18). Paul wrote a letter to Titus in order "that they which have believed in God might be careful to maintain good works" (Titus 3:8). In sum, we cannot be holy by our own efforts, but we can be holy if we put our faith in Jesus and let His Spirit work in us.

Jesus came to deliver us from the law and its orientation toward works. He also delivered us from bondage to sin. We are no longer servants of sin or the law, but we are free to make godly choices. We are free to say no to sin and say yes to God's will.

We have liberty in Christ, but we must not use that liberty to indulge in fleshly activities or harm someone else. "For, brethren, ye have been called unto liberty; only use not liberty for an occasion to the flesh, but by love serve one another" (Galatians 5:13). We are no longer under the law, but if we walk after the Spirit we will fulfill the righteousness that the law taught but could not impart. Before Christ, people tried to fulfill the law by their own efforts, but they failed because they were weak in the flesh and subject to sin. After Christ, we are set free from the dominion of sin, and through the power of the Spirit we can overcome the weakness of the flesh. We are able to follow the Spirit, thereby fulfilling the righteousness of the law (Romans 8:1-4).

The work of the Spirit. The Spirit baptizes us into the body of Christ (I Corinthians 12:13) and adopts us into the family of God (Romans 8:15-16). In other words, the Spirit gives us a new identity. We are transformed by the indwelling Spirit of Christ—Christ in us (Romans 8:9; Colossians 1:27). We put on the mind of Christ (I Corinthians 2:16; Philippians 2:5). Christ is formed in us (Galatians 4:19). The Spirit of God conforms us to the image of Christ (Romans 8:29). We are able to live holy lives by letting the mind, personality, and will of Jesus Christ supersede our own. Jesus lived on the earth for thirty-three years to give us an example to follow (I Peter 2:21-24). He died and rose again to defeat sin and death and to give us power to follow His example (Romans 8:3-4).

Holiness means letting the Spirit and personality of Christ shine through us. We want to display His Spirit. We want to please Him and be like Him. We want to live as He lived and do what He would do. We want to manifest the characteristics and traits of Jesus Christ. In this way we become living examples of Christianity. We become open letters from Christ to the world, written by the Spirit (II Corinthians 3:2-3). The good works that He produces in us will lead people to God, and they will glorify Him (Matthew 5:16).

Christian characteristics. What are the characteristics that Christians (Christ-like people) display? Galatians 5:22-23 gives us an excellent list, called the fruit of the Spirit. If we have the Spirit in us, we will bear this fruit. While speaking in other tongues is the initial evidence of receiving the Holy Spirit, the abiding evidence that the Holy Spirit dwells in a life is the manifestation of the fruit of the Spirit. Paul listed nine aspects of spiritual fruit: love, joy, peace, longsuffering, gentleness, goodness, faith, meekness, and temperance. Peter listed eight qualities that will make us fruitful in Christ: faith, virtue, knowledge, temperance, patience, godliness, brotherly kindness, and charity (II Peter 1:5-10). Faith and temperance are repeated in both lists. Virtue and godliness are aspects of goodness, brotherly kindness and charity are aspects of love, and patience is similar to longsuffering. Peter also noted some characteristics of Christ for us to imitate (I Peter 2:21-24). The passage explains that Christ had no sin or guile (deceit) and describes His love, patience, temperance, and faith while suffering for our sins.

We will be dealing with all these attitudes and characteristics throughout the book. In order to lay a foundation we want to discuss briefly the ninefold fruit of the Spirit as listed in Galatians. This is the fruit God wants us to bear, and this is the fruit that will attract sinners to the gospel message.

Love. Love is the most basic element of our Christian life. It is the only acceptable motivation for serving God. We are commanded to love our fellow Christians, to love our neighbors, and even to love our enemies. If we do not love our fellow humans, then we do not love God. If we love the world, then we do not love God. Love is the test of true Christianity.

If we understand what love really means, we can fulfill the Bible's teaching on holiness. For example, love one for another will eliminate jealousy, strife, talebearing, complaining, and bitterness. Love for God will eliminate worldliness and rebellion. On the other hand, if we do not love both God and people then nothing will make us right in the sight of God. Correct doctrines and good works cannot take the place of love. The closer to God we become, the more love we will have. "The love of God is shed abroad in our hearts by the Holy Ghost" (Romans 5:5).

(For further discussion, with scriptural references, see chapter 3.)

Joy. As with the other aspects of spiritual fruit, we receive joy from the Holy Spirit (Romans 14:17). Our experience with God is "joy unspeakable and full of glory" (I Peter 1:8). We can have God's joy no matter what happens to us. This joy is different from what the world gives, for it is not dependent on circumstances. Regardless of external conditions, we can always rejoice in our salvation and in the God of our salvation (Luke 10:20; Habakkuk 3:17-18). Joy is a weapon and a source of strength. "The joy of the LORD is your strength" (Nehemiah 8:10). When discouragement comes, we can draw upon the joy of the Spirit. The way to overcome in time of trial is to "count it all joy when ye fall into divers temptations" (James 1:2). We can praise our way to victory.

How do we obtain joy in time of need? Our salvation itself is a source of joy. "Therefore with joy shall ye draw water out of the wells of salvation. And in that day shall ye say, Praise the LORD" (Isaiah 12:3-4). Psalms tells us about two other sources of joy. "They that sow in tears shall reap in joy" (Psalm 126:5). If we plant good seed with tears and prayers, we will reap good results with joy. "In thy presence is fulness of joy" (Psalm 16:11). When we draw close to God and enter into His presence, we have perfect joy. We can enter into His presence with singing, thanksgiving, and praise (Psalm 100).

Peace. We also have peace in the Holy Spirit—peace that passes all understanding and peace about which the world knows nothing (Romans 14:17; Philippians 4:7). No matter what happens, we can have inner peace. Jesus said, "Peace I leave with you, my peace I give unto you:

not as the world giveth, give I unto you. Let not your heart be troubled, neither let it be afraid" (John 14:27).

Not only can we have peace of mind but also peace with others. In fact, God expects this of us. "Follow peace with all men" (Hebrews 12:14). (See also Romans 12:18.) Jesus said, "Blessed are the peacemakers"—those who make peace where there is no peace, those who bring peace to a troubled person or a troubled situation (Matthew 5:9).

How can we acquire and maintain peace in our lives? We will have perfect peace if we focus our minds on God and trust Him. "Thou wilt keep him in perfect peace, whose mind is stayed on thee: because he trusteth in thee" (Isaiah 26:3). We experience peace as we rejoice in the Lord, live in moderation (gentleness), lay aside anxiety, and make our requests known to God through prayer and supplication with thanksgiving (Philippians 4:4-7).

Longsuffering and patience. Patience is important in our Christian experience. Jesus said, "In your patience possess ye your souls" (Luke 21:19). We bear fruit with patience (Luke 8:15), we run our race with patience (Hebrews 12:1), and we obtain promises by faith and patience (Hebrews 6:12). "For ye have need of patience, that, after ye have done the will of God, ye might receive the promise" (Hebrews 10:36).

Longsuffering connotes patience or forbearance in relationships with people. Paul implored us to walk worthy of our calling, "with all lowliness and meekness, with longsuffering, forbearing one another in love; endeavouring to keep the unity of the Spirit in the bond of peace" (Ephesians 4:2-3). Longsuffering comes with meekness, love, a desire for unity, and a desire for peace. Patience comes by the trying of faith and by tribulation (Romans 5:3; James 1:3). If we let patience have its perfect work, we will have experience, hope, and everything else that we need (Romans 5:4; James 1:4).

Gentleness. Gentleness is not the same as weakness. To be gentle is to be courteous, mannerly, kind, patient, serene, and not harsh, violent, or rough. Jesus was gentle in dealing with people, yet He was firm and decisive when necessary. The Lord wants us to be gentle toward everyone (II Timothy 2:24). His gentleness will make us great (Psalm 18:35).

Goodness. This word includes righteousness, morality, virtue, and excellence. We must remember that "there is none good but one, that is, God" (Mark 10:18). Any good thing we have comes from Him (James 1:17). All our righteousness is as filthy rags in His sight (Isaiah 64:6); only the righteousness of Christ saves us. When we have faith in Jesus, we receive His righteousness (Romans 4:5-6). We are saved as we continue in God's goodness (Romans 11:22).

Faith. Not only do we need faith to be saved, but we need faith to continue our Christian walk. Without faith it is impossible to please God (Hebrews 11:6). Faith causes us to realize that all things work together for good to those who love God (Romans 8:28). Faith assures us that God will never allow us to be tempted more than we can bear and that He will always provide a way of escape (I Corinthians 10:13). Faith results in answered prayer, supplied needs, and fulfilled promises. "And all things, whatsoever ye shall ask in prayer, believing, ye shall receive" (Matthew 21:22). (See also Mark 11:22-24.) This aspect of spiritual fruit involves faithfulness, which means being loyal, true, constant, and consistent.

How do we receive faith? God has given a measure of faith to everyone (Romans 12:3). Surely we have as much faith as a grain of mustard seed, and if we will exercise this much faith, nothing will be impossible (Matthew 17:20). "Faith cometh by hearing, and hearing by the word of God" (Romans 10:17). We build faith primarily by hearing the preaching and teaching of God's Word and by reading the promises of God's Word. We can also increase our faith by hearing the testimonies of others and by drawing upon our own past experiences with God. Faith can also come in a critical moment as a supernatural gift of the Spirit (I Corinthians 12:9).

Meekness. To be meek means to be patient, mild, and not inclined to anger or resentment. It does not mean weakness or spinelessness. Meekness includes humility—a realization that we are nothing without God and that we must have His help. Meekness is an important quality for leaders to have. Moses was the meekest man in his day (Numbers 12:3), and Jesus described Himself as meek and lowly (Matthew 11:29). Jesus said that the meek would inherit the earth (Matthew 5:5). The Lord wants us to show meekness to everyone (Titus 3:2).

Here are some things the Bible says should be done with meekness: preaching the Word (II Corinthians 10:1), receiving the Word (James 1:21), helping and restoring an erring brother (Galatians 6:1), displaying wisdom (James 3:13), and adorning our lives (I Peter 3:4). Meekness is an attitude that we must consciously develop in ourselves. It takes effort on our part. "Submit yourselves therefore to God. . . . Humble yourselves in the sight of the Lord" (James 4:7, 10).

Temperance encompasses self-restraint, self-control, and moderation. Any pleasure can become painful if carried to excess, and any good thing can be ruined by taking it to extremes. In I Corinthians 9:24-27 Paul illustrated the concept of temperance by a runner in a race. To win, runners must be "temperate in all things." They must have discipline and self-control. They must have a well-balanced training program and must be moderate in their activities. Likewise, Paul had discipline and control. He knew what his goal was, and he kept his body under subjection. Temperance or self-control is an attribute that we need to display at all times.

Wisdom in dealing with people. It is important to emphasize the principles of this chapter when teaching, preaching, and talking to people about matters of practical holiness. Pastors especially need wisdom in this area. We err if we equate Christianity with rules. As Christians we follow God's commands because we want to please Him and not because someone forces us to do them. Holiness is positive. It means having Christ-like qualities, bearing the fruit of the Spirit, exercising the power of the Spirit, and being free from the bondage of sin.

We personally have strong holiness convictions, as this book discusses, and we do not advocate compromise of them. Much harm has been done by those who do not teach on holiness and those who change their beliefs under pressure from the world. However, much harm has also been done under the guise of holiness teaching by those who emphasize negatives, prohibitions, and rules and by those who lack wisdom in dealing with visitors and new converts.

As a general rule, preachers should proclaim the basic themes of holiness in their messages and emphasize the positive nature of the gospel. They should not preach on matters of practical holiness with vehement condemnation but should teach on these subjects with love, patience, and understanding. We should follow the approach of the New Testament itself. For example, we can exhort people to follow modesty and temperance and to avoid sins such as lying and fornication. Specific problem areas can be handled by personal counseling and exhortation.

We need to welcome visitors and love them as they are. We are not to judge or condemn but allow God to bring conviction. It takes the Holy Spirit to draw people to repentance and to give them power to change their way of life.

Individual believers should avoid telling visitors and newcomers what to do. If they ask questions, believers can give them scriptural answers and refer them to the pastor in delicate situations. If they are in the process of repenting, the pastor may need to advise them about sin in their lives. However, they can immediately receive the Holy Spirit if we will stress repentance, faith, a willingness to change, and a desire to do God's will. If they manifest these attitudes they can be filled even though they do not yet have an understanding of certain issues and doctrines. After they receive the Holy Spirit, it will be much easier for them to sort out problems, learn about God, and clean up their lives.

In working with new converts, it is important to have patience and tolerance. They need much positive teaching, encouragement, and understanding. They need to learn how to be sensitive to the Spirit and how to rely upon the Spirit to overcome trials and temptations. Many people have received a genuine experience from God but were driven away from the church by harshness, intolerance, overzealous admonition, and lack of wisdom. They choked on meat that was forced on them when they needed milk and time to grow. (See I Corinthians 3:2; Hebrews 5:12.) We must give God time to work on them through His Spirit, the preaching of the Word, and the example of the congregation.

If it is necessary for a pastor to deal with a specific situation, it is wise to use suggestions instead of commands. It is better to explain why a course of action is beneficial instead of using threats or coercion. Let us never underestimate the power of God to change lives. A good way to teach converts is to enroll them in a discipleship class. The teacher explains the principles of Christian living, answers all questions courteously, and uses the Bible rather than tradition as the authority. When people are ready to become voting members, teachers, ushers, choir members, or worship leaders, the pastor can ask them to meet certain qualifications.

Pastors can usually deal with individual problems or concerns through private discussion. To establish clear guidelines, it is advisable to have a saints' meeting (a closed meeting for church members with an alternate class provided for visitors and newcomers). Meetings with the choir, Sunday school staff, and other ministry positions can also be good opportunities to provide specific instructions. If corrective action must be taken in a particular situation, it is usually best to do so quietly and individually. In this way, the pastor can maintain high standards for the church and at the same time avoid confusion for visitors and new converts.

Holiness as a way of life. In the final analysis, we can only give suggestions and advice based on prayer, biblical study, and experience. God gives each individual the privilege and responsibility to respond according to his or her own conscience. Of course, we are all responsible to obey the clear teachings of Scripture regardless of personal opinions and desires.

The Christian life is a personal relationship with God. It is a continual search for holiness as we draw close to God and become more like Him. If we will let His Spirit lead us and if we will cultivate the fruit of the Spirit, then the pursuit of holiness will not be difficult. It will be a joy and not a burden. It will be a normal way of life.

CHAPTER

3

Christian Attitudes

Let all bitterness, and wrath, and anger, and clamour, and evil speaking, be put away from you, with all malice: and be ye kind one to another, tenderhearted, forgiving one another, even as God for Christ's sake hath forgiven you (Ephesians 4:31-32).

Attitudes are the most important elements of holiness. If we have the proper attitude toward God and our fellow humans, we will manifest holiness in all areas of life. If we do not have the right attitude, no amount of outward holiness will compensate for the lack of inward holiness in the sight of God. Wrong attitudes are the first signs of backsliding and are inevitable components of hypocrisy.

Love is the basic attitude that distinguishes true Christians from the world. We can sum up all the law and prophets in two commandments: Love God and love our fellow humans (Matthew 22:36-40; Mark 12:28-31; Luke 10:27). Love will cause us to keep God's commandments (John 14:15, 23). In fact, we demonstrate our love for God by how faithfully we obey His Word (I John 2:3-5).

Jesus commanded that we love one another even as He has loved us (John 15:12, 17). Love one to another is the ultimate test of true Christianity (John 13:34-35). If we do not love our brothers and sisters then we do not love God (I John 4:20-21). Love is the fulfillment of the law (Leviticus 19:18; Romans 13:10; James 2:8). God calls Christians to extend love to every human being, even enemies (Matthew 5:43-48). Once again, this type of love is the ultimate proof of Christianity, for even sinners love those who love them in return (Matthew 5:46).

We cannot overemphasize the necessity of love as the basis for all actions and all relationships. Love never fails (I Corinthians 13:8). We will not fail God or each other if we let love have its perfect work. No activity or attribute is worth anything if love is not the underlying force and motivating factor (I Corinthians 13:1-3; Revelation 2:1-5). The preceding passages list the following things that are valueless without love: speaking in tongues, eloquence, prophecy, wisdom, knowledge, faith, sacrifice, philanthropy, works, labor, patience, right doctrine, right leadership, right fellowship, perseverance, and zeal for Jesus' name.

Let us apply these teachings about love to the subject of holiness. First, we should love God enough to do His perfect will. If we love Him as we should, we will want to be like Him as much as possible. We will try to avoid anything that is not like Him. We will want to please Him even in areas that from a human viewpoint might seem to be unnecessary or trivial. If we begin to question holiness teachings, we should check to see how deep our love for God really is.

Second, we should be on guard when any type of resentment or dislike arises in us toward another human being. We must retain a loving and forgiving attitude toward that person if we want to maintain our holiness and our Christianity. Love for others means we are patient, kind, not envious, not egotistical, not boastful, mannerly, not self-seeking, not easily provoked, slow to think evil of someone, and pleased only with what is good. Love bears all things, believes all things, hopes all things, and endures all things (I Corinthians 13:4-7). Our actions must be motivated by this kind of love for God and our fellow humans. Following holiness teachings for any other reason or without this love is worthless and will lead to hypocrisy.

Having established the importance of right attitudes, let us examine some specific teachings concerning them. Ephesians 4:31, quoted at the beginning of this chapter, lists some dangerous attitudes that Christians must put away. If we allow these attitudes to remain in our lives, we will feed the flesh and starve our spiritual life.

Bitterness is something sharp, disagreeable, distasteful, harsh, severe, resentful, or vehement. This type of attitude produces piercing remarks and unpleasant language. It is never appropriate. Some people think they can put aside their spirituality and give vent to their bitterness, but they cannot do so if they want to be holy. Even when leaders issue necessary rebukes, they must not do so with personal bitterness or with sharp, disagreeable, harsh, severe words. There is a time for rebuke and exhortation but never with bitterness.

Wrath is violent anger, rage, or indignation; the word suggests a desire to avenge or punish. The flesh wants to get revenge, and it often does so by a display of harsh feelings or a cutting remark. We may disagree on certain issues, but we must not become resentful or vengeful. We may be perfectly correct in principle, but if we allow ourselves to become violently angry or wrathful then we are wrong. The same is true about the other wrong attitudes we are discussing. We cannot allow ourselves to be ungoverned, but we must learn to control our feelings. Instead of relying upon our own strength, we control wrath through prayer and seeking God.

It is especially disgraceful for a minister to become violently angry or resentful, even with regard to the work of the church. There is no way to explain this lack of control to followers. We must remember that "the wrath of man worketh not the righteousness of God" (James 1:20).

Anger is a feeling of extreme displeasure that usually results from injury or opposition. The word itself does not suggest a definite degree of intensity, nor does it necessarily require an outward manifestation. If anger is allowed to go uncontrolled, it usually manifests itself as a desire to lash out at someone or something. If controlled and used properly, anger may be constructive and even beneficial. For example, Jesus displayed anger against sin when He cleansed the Temple of thieves. Thus, anger itself is not sinful, but in many situations it can easily lead to sin.

What kind of anger is permissible and what is not? "Be ye angry, and sin not: let not the sun go down upon your wrath" (Ephesians 4:26). Anger that causes us to harm someone in word or deed is wrong. Anger that we carry in our heart and nurse into a grudge is also wrong. Anger without a cause is wrong (Matthew 5:22).

If there is a just cause for anger, we should not take the situation personally and we should not direct that anger against an individual to hurt him or her. Instead, we should use the emotional force as a motivation to correct the wrong if possible. Then, we should forgive the other individual involved and pray until the situation no longer has power over us. Regardless of the circumstances, temperance or self-control is part of the fruit of the Spirit that we should display (Galatians 5:23).

What should be the attitude of pastors when some people in the church live in disobedience to God's Word? They should not react in personal anger but should maintain self-control, recognizing that the people are not rebelling against them personally but against God.

Clamor is noisy shouting, outcry, uproar, or insistent demand. Some people constantly complain. They clamor to get their way. Some adults throw temper tantrums and act as stubborn as small children who fall on the floor, scream, and kick. People who keep the church in an uproar—constantly demanding attention, always presenting demands, or blocking the progress of the church—are guilty of clamor. Scripture condemns this attitude and behavior.

Evil speaking comes from an evil heart. Much of it stems from jealousy. Do we allow ourselves to speak evil of people? Do we cause trouble by our speech? (See chapter 4 for further discussion of talebearing and reviling.)

Malice is active ill will, a desire to hurt others. Malice takes pleasure in causing someone to suffer or in seeing someone suffer. It is usually the result of hatred, which is like the sin of murder in the eyes of God (I John 3:15). We should hate sin but not the sinner. We can rejoice when sin is defeated but never in the misfortunes and sufferings of other people, even if they are sinners. Love does not rejoice in iniquity but only in the truth (I Corinthians 13:6).

Envy and jealousy. These emotions are closely associated with bitterness, wrath, malice, and strife. Envy is resentment or ill will because of the advantages, possessions, or accomplishments of someone else. Jealousy is a resentful suspicion or envy. These attitudes often involve spite or greed.

Envy and strife are capable of producing any and every kind of evil (James 3:16). Envy is a work of the flesh that prevents people from going to heaven (Galatians 5:21; James 4:5). This spirit surfaces unexpectedly in places where it should not be. People may get upset when someone else is used more in the church, is recognized more than they, receives certain favors, or even receives spiritual blessings.

Forgiveness. In place of all evil attitudes, Scripture exhorts us to be kind to one another, tenderhearted and forgiving. Forgiveness is based on love and involves bearing the cost of someone else's mistake. It means giving up our rights in certain situations and ignoring certain things even when we know we are correct. It means swallowing our pride and asking others to forgive us even when we think they should be asking our pardon instead. It means turning the other cheek (Matthew 5:39).

Most importantly, forgiveness includes a decision to forget. Some people say, "I'll forgive, but I won't forget."

They need to pray until they *can* forget; that is, until they no longer hold anything against someone. Some people pretend to forget but bring up an old grudge at a future confrontation. Or they may bring up an old mistake in order to gain some advantage over someone. This is not true forgiveness.

Forgiveness does not mean saying someone is right when they have done evil or saying their actions do not matter. Nor does it mean making ourselves vulnerable to those who have harmed us, thereby enabling them to harm us again. But it does mean refusing to retaliate with evil and refusing to harbor bitterness. It means putting the past behind us and being willing to accept sincere repentance.

Jesus plainly taught that God will forgive us only as much as we forgive others (Matthew 6:12, 14-15; 18:23-35). If we want to be forgiven of our sins, we must learn to forgive our brothers and sisters when they make mistakes.

A root of bitterness. Some people seemingly can never be satisfied. They murmur, complain, refuse to cooperate, and are self-willed. They cannot accept correction without becoming angry. They are busybodies, they sow discord in the church, they are talebearers, and they cause problems everywhere they go. What is wrong? It could be that they have a root of bitterness. "Looking diligently lest any man fail of the grace of God; lest any root of bitterness springing up trouble you, and thereby many be defiled" (Hebrews 12:15).

Significantly, this statement comes immediately after the admonition to follow peace and holiness (verse 14). In other words, bitterness will defile our holiness. The implication is that having a proper attitude is the most important aspect of holiness.

A root of bitterness is a source of bitterness. It is something in the heart that causes the outward manifestations we have identified. From this root many types of fruit come forth, none of which is the fruit of the Spirit. The actual root could be a grudge, jealousy, a wrong done to us that we have not turned over to God, or something else in our heart that we have never surrendered to God. If we develop a bad attitude, we should check for a source of bitterness in our heart. We must cut it out and destroy it so that we can bear enjoyable fruit.

We do not have the authority to judge the motives or heart of others, but we can observe fruit. If we see an apple growing on a tree, we know that it is an apple tree. The fruit speaks for itself. Likewise, when someone has a root of bitterness, the fruit will be easy to observe. Without attempting to judge the person, we can know enough to avoid participating in the gossip, envy, hatred, and strife that come out of that source. We can refuse to partake of such fruit, lest we be one of the many who are defiled by that person's root of bitterness.

Nothing shall offend. The Christian's attitude stands in stark contrast to the root of bitterness and all of its resulting attitudes. "Great peace have they which love thy law: and nothing shall offend them" (Psalm 119:165). Peace is the result of loving God and His Word (Philippians 4:7). Peace is one of the results of being justified (counted as righteous in the sight of God) (Romans 5:1).

An offense is something that causes a person to stumble in his or her walk with God. God's Word teaches us not to let anything offend us (cause us to stumble) and not to offend others (cause others to stumble). (See Matthew 5:29-30; 13:41; James 3:2.) Nothing will be a stumbling block to those who love the Word of God.

We sometimes hear complaints such as the following: "They invited others, but they did not invite me." "They asked others to do something at church but not me." "They never ask me to participate." "I was entitled to a certain thing because of my position or age, but they did not give it to me." "They did not speak to me." How many times have our feelings been hurt because we were rebuked, misunderstood, or overlooked? In all these cases, let us remember: "Nothing shall offend." Perhaps there were good reasons for a certain action that we do not know about, perhaps we did not get the true story, or perhaps someone made a mistake.

Regardless of the circumstances, we cannot allow ourselves to develop a bad attitude or lose our faith in God and in the church. We need an attitude of forgiveness when it appears that others have mistreated us—even if they do not ask forgiveness. When we pray the Lord's Prayer, we ask God to forgive us as much as we forgive others! (See Matthew 6:12-15.) Even when there is a violation of custom or etiquette, and even if we are in the right, we cannot allow ourselves to develop a bitter, unforgiving spirit. If we love God, then we will not let anything become a stumbling block to us. No matter what happens, we will not stumble and fall.

It may seem humanly impossible to respond positively to negative situations, but God gives us the power to overcome. Instead of complaining, "I am offended," or "Someone hurt my feelings," let us pray until God gives us victory in every situation.

Attitude when corrected. We must maintain this determination in times of rebuke or reproof. "Shew me thy ways, O LORD; teach me thy paths" (Psalm 25:4). Some people think they never need instruction, correction, rebuke, reproof, or exhortation. But the Word of God says we do. God has placed government in the church, and everyone from the highest in position to the lowest is subject to godly authority. (See chapter 12.) Even Peter and Paul accepted rebuke from others (Galatians 2:11-14; Acts 23:3-5). People who do not wish to submit to spiritual authority are on their way to apostasy (II Peter 2:10).

Let us never esteem ourselves so highly that we cannot accept admonition, rebuke, or exhortation. When someone in spiritual authority admonishes us out of love and faithfulness, we should carefully consider the admonition with the attitude of "Thank you for trying to help me"—not "I'm just as spiritual as you are, and you have made mistakes too, so I don't need to listen to you."

Hebrews 13:17 says, "Obey them that have the rule over you, and submit yourselves: for they watch for your souls, as they that must give account, that they may do it with joy, and not with grief: for that is unprofitable for you." This admonition applies to all believers, including leaders, and it teaches some important principles. First, God has ordained leaders in the church. He has organized a system of church government. Second, we are to be humble and obedient. "To obey is better than sacrifice. . . . For rebellion is as the sin of witchcraft" (I Samuel 15:22-23). Third, true leaders have a duty to watch over our souls. If they see something sinful or dangerous, they have an obligation to warn us. We should accept their warning without becoming angry, for they are merely fulfilling their duty. Fourth, leaders are responsible to God. Whether they warn us or not is between them and God. Whether we listen and submit is between us and God. Finally, God will be our judge, and all rebellion against His authority will be unprofitable for us.

"A reproof entereth more into a wise man than an hundred stripes into a fool" (Proverbs 17:10). If we are wise, we will accept reproof. Just a few words of admonition are sufficient if we have the proper attitude. If we think we are beyond reproof, then we place ourselves in the position of a scoffer or a wicked person. If we are wise, we will love the godly leader or friend who rebukes us. (See Proverbs 9:7-9.) Both those giving a rebuke and receiving a rebuke must have the proper attitude in order for there to be good results.

Can a leader be rebuked? Nothing in Scripture suggests that a minister or other leader is exempt from these guidelines. Of course, the rebuke must come from someone with the proper spiritual authority. Even elders (pastors) who live in sin should be rebuked before others, so that everyone may learn (I Timothy 5:20). Unfortunately, when some are rebuked they receive so much sympathy and comfort from "friends" that they do not repent but instead become rebellious. In this case, no one learns what God intended.

"All scripture is given by inspiration of God, and is profitable for doctrine, for reproof, for correction, for instruction in righteousness. . . . Preach the word; be instant in season, out of season; reprove, rebuke, exhort with all longsuffering and doctrine" (II Timothy 3:16; 4:2). Preachers are authorized, and indeed commanded, to use the Word to reprove (correct or convince), rebuke, and exhort (encourage). Consequently, let us always have the proper attitude when we receive admonition. Let us pray, "Show me your ways, Lord. Lead me. When I stray, send someone or something to correct me before it is too late. Help me to have a good attitude when I listen to messages or even to personal admonition. Help me not to make excuses, justify myself, or rebel against godly authority, but teach me to obey. Give me leaders who love me enough to teach me the truth and correct me when I need it."

Murmuring and complaining. According to Jude 15-16, those who murmur (grumble) and complain (find fault) are ungodly. When differences arise, Christians are to pray for one another and encourage one another, not attack one another. "Do all things without murmurings and disputings" (Philippians 2:14). If there is a problem between two people, they should seek reconciliation without spreading the problem to others (Matthew 18:15). Instead, if they complain and murmur by talking or writing, they can become guilty of sowing discord. (See chapter 4.)

It does not take much to tempt the average person or congregation to complain. Small inconveniences or the temporary lack of water, food, clothing, or money will test everyone. If we do not allow God to guide us, we easily become prisoners of our desires, appetites, and passions.

The Israelites, for example, began to complain about everything in the second month of their journey through the wilderness (Exodus 16:1-3). In Exodus alone we find twelve major complaints of Israel against God's plan and God's chosen leader. Their complaining stemmed from unbelief and a lack of respect for God's appointed leadership. Because of their unbelief they ended up traveling for forty years on a journey that should have taken only a few months.

Jude 11 teaches us to avoid the rebellion of Korah. This man criticized Moses and challenged his spiritual authority. Consequently, God caused the earth to swallow him and his followers. When Miriam and Aaron criticized Moses, the Lord heard it (Numbers 12:2). Although Miriam and Aaron were the older siblings of Moses, God rebuked them just the same. "Were ye not afraid to speak against my servant?" God asked (Numbers 12:8). Miriam was stricken with leprosy for seven days as punishment for her sin.

Paul learned "in whatsoever state I am, therewith to be content" (Philippians 4:11). When we feel mistreated, the solution is not to murmur and complain. Rather, we will find our answer through prayer. If applicable and necessary, we should talk directly to the person who has created the unpleasant situation. But we should not seek to avenge ourselves, for that prerogative belongs to God alone (Romans 12:19).

We find an excellent example of the proper attitude in David's relationship to Saul. Saul clearly wronged David, even trying to take his life. Saul had sinned to the point where God rejected him, and Samuel had already anointed David to be the next king. Yet, on two occasions, David refused to kill Saul when he had the chance to do so. As long as Saul was king, David did not want to harm him. David waited for God to remove Saul.

Instead of grumbling and finding fault, let us learn to be content, to pray, and to talk about situations to the right people with the right attitude. There is no use in confronting a matter if we cannot speak with a humble, quiet, forgiving spirit.

Complaining is contagious. It is also contrary to the Word of the Lord.

Busybodies. In addition to having a proper relationship with leaders, we need a proper relationship with fellow believers. Busybodies are inquisitive about other people's personal affairs, meddlers in the business of others, people who are busy with matters that should not concern them. I Peter 4:15 tells us not to suffer "as a busybody in other men's matters." Paul also warned against busybodies (II Thessalonians 3:11; I Timothy 5:13). According to Proverbs 20:3, a meddler is a fool.

Busybodies seem to know a little about everyone else's business and involve themselves in all kinds of problems. Often they try to interfere with the disciplining of an individual and try to "solve problems" without working with the pastor. Most of the time they do not help, but they just add more wood to the fire. Such people are a curse to a neighborhood and a plague to a church. These people try to find out everything that is going on. They feel that they are important and that they know everything. Actually they cannot be trusted with any important job that requires keeping things in confidence. As a result, a busybody does not qualify for the ministry.

We should examine ourselves to see if we have the tendency to be a busybody. If we are inquisitive by nature, we must let the Holy Spirit deliver us from excessive curiosity concerning other people's lives.

Pride. God hates a proud look (Proverbs 6:17). He resists the proud but gives grace to the humble (James

4:6). Pride was the sin that caused Satan to fall, and it will cause the downfall and destruction of all who harbor it (Isaiah 14:12-15; Proverbs 16:18). The pride of life is one of the three basic categories of worldliness that tempt Christians (I John 2:16). John the Baptist and Jesus preached their harshest sermons against the hypocrisy and pride of religious people. Remarkably, they did not direct these vehement statements at the acknowledged sinners but at the spiritual leaders of their day. Clearly, religious people are susceptible to the sin of pride.

When talking about holiness, it is easy to become self-righteous and critical of others. It is possible to look holy but to be full of pride and hypocrisy, and in such a case we will not be justified in the sight of God. As an example, God rejected the pious prayer of a self-righteous Pharisee but heard the sincere cry of repentance from a sinful tax collector (Luke 18:9-14).

We must not let pride enter our hearts because we know truth and follow after holiness. Nor can we allow ourselves to develop the appearance of pride.

Preachers are susceptible in both areas. Since God hates a proud look, we should be careful how we conduct ourselves. Do we manifest pride in the way we speak to believers, in the way we sit on the platform, or even in the way we walk around with our Bibles?

No matter how spiritually mature we may be, we must always guard against pride. The more successful we are spiritually, the more the devil would like to tempt us with pride. We must seek after humility.

Even in this pursuit we must be careful, for some people try so hard to display humility that they actually appear to take pride in their so-called humility. True humility neither exalts nor disparages self but is not preoccupied with self. If we think we are very humble, then most likely we are not. If we rejoice in the attainment of great humility, then probably we have just lost it.

We can eradicate pride through prayer—the kind of prayer in which we fall down on our faces before God, lie prostrate before Him, and weep in His presence. We examine our hearts, and we ask God to reveal to us our true motives and attitudes. As we confess our faults, failures, inadequacies, and sins, we recognize the depth of our unworthiness and the magnitude of God's mercy and grace. This kind of prayer is not counted in minutes but in hours. After our spirit is broken and pride is washed away, then we can receive precious blessings and anointing from God. Such an experience is not something to boast of to others but to hide in our hearts. By periodically renewing this type of experience, we can guard against pride.

The feminist movement. Some things about the feminist movement are consistent with the Word of God, but some things are not. On the positive side, the Bible teaches that women and men are equal in importance and value. They are potentially equal in talent, intelligence, and spiritual gifts. There is no unequal treatment of male and female in Christ (Galatians 3:28). Throughout the Bible, God used women as prophetesses, judges, teachers, deaconesses, and laborers in the gospel. (See Judges 4:4; Isaiah 8:3; Acts 18:26; 21:9; Romans 16:1; Philippians 4:3.) Applying these principles to daily life, women and men deserve equal pay for equal performance of the same job.

At the same time, the roles of wife and husband are

different, and so are the roles of mother and father. The Bible teaches mutual submission to one another, and it also teaches that the wife should follow the godly leadership of her own husband. (See Ephesians 5:21-22; Colossians 3:18; I Peter 3:1.) God has given the husband the primary responsibility of providing for his family and leading them in righteousness. Along with that responsibility comes the authority to fulfill this role.

The husband is to love his wife as Christ loves the church and to treat her kindly (Ephesians 5:25; Colossians 3:19). He is to honor and respect her; otherwise, his prayers will be hindered (I Peter 3:7).

The ancient Jewish rabbis pointed out that in the Genesis account the woman came from the side of the man, not from his head or his feet. Thus, they explained, she is not to lead him, nor is he to dominate her, but he should cherish her by his side. She is a helper comparable to and suitable for him; husband and wife complement each other (Genesis 2:18). A wife's first responsibility is to help her husband and care for her children. The Bible strongly advocates marriage and the home, while condemning extramarital sexual relationships, homosexuality, and lesbianism. (See chapter 9.)

Can any man assert authority over any woman? No. A man is the leader of his own home, and a woman should respect the leadership of her own husband. Beyond that, general principles of leadership and authority apply.

In the early church, women prayed and prophesied publicly (Acts 2:17; 21:9; I Corinthians 11:5; 14:31). However, they were not to interrupt a public assembly to ask questions—a privilege that men often had in those days (I Corinthians 14:34-35). In the New Testament, women functioned in leadership and ministry roles (Romans 16:1-12). However, they were not to usurp authority but fulfilled leadership and teaching roles under the authority of men (I Timothy 2:11-12).

In spiritual matters, a woman should follow the leadership of her husband as he follows the Lord. Even if he is not a Christian, she should acknowledge him as the leader of the family in order to win him to God (I Peter 3:1-2). On matters of personal conviction, doctrine, and spiritual experience, a woman must be true to her own individual beliefs since God ultimately will judge everyone on an individual basis.

Church meetings. Chapter 12 discusses church organization, government, and authority more fully, but in this section we discuss the proper attitude in church meetings. At the first general conference of the church (Acts 15), an important, controversial issue was decided—namely, what practices of the Jewish law are mandatory for Gentile Christians. Delegates came to Jerusalem, where they met with the apostles and elders (pastors) there (verses 2-4). Both sides debated and disputed at great length, with the major views being fully represented (verse 7). Finally, they reached a decision, which everyone agreed to support. They sent letters to the various congregations informing them of this decision (15:23; 16:4).

We should notice that the leaders of the church worked together after the decision despite the sharp differences of opinion that had originally existed. They also worked together in sending letters of recommendation and collecting special offerings (Acts 18:27; II Corinthians 8:19). They loved each other, helped each other, and even rebuked each other when they saw the need. Paul rebuked Peter and others "when I saw that they walked not uprightly according to the truth of the gospel" (Galatians 2:14).

What took place in Acts 15 was a democratic discussion in which a strong majority of the elders formulated a decision under the influence of the Holy Spirit (verse 28). After this conference, the church united in support of the decision. Democracy does not mean doing whatever we choose and never listening to someone else, but it means following the majority on nonessential, nondoctrinal matters. When a majority makes a decision, we should accept the decision with a good attitude, without murmuring, complaining, or sowing discord.

If we have confidence in our leaders and fellow ministers, then it is easy to believe that God can influence a majority of them in the right direction. If we love our fellow believers, we can accede to the wishes of the majority. At the same time, the leaders must not have an attitude of pride that says, "I am the leader, so you do as I say." Ministers are not lords over God's heritage but examples to the flock (I Peter 5:3). All of us should manifest brotherly and sisterly love, "in honour preferring one another" (Romans 12:10).

What should a business meeting or a conference be like? The participants should not speak with anger, resentment, or bitterness. How can we act in this manner and at the same time inspire others? How can we exercise the ministry of reconciliation if we cannot get along with each other? A conference is a time to conduct business but also a time for fellowship, healing, renewal, and the outpouring of the Holy Spirit. It should be a time for strengthening convictions and listening to others proclaim the message that we love. It is refreshing to hear someone else explain the truth in such a way that we can say, "This is what I believe, too." Conferences are times for mutual encouragement, not for talebearing, murmuring, complaining, or disputing.

In the business of the church, let us guard against a stubborn attitude. It should be a warning if we find ourselves saying, "Well, I'll just do it anyway"; "If they don't do it my way, I won't participate"; or "I don't need anyone to tell me what to do."

The most important aspect of holiness. In conclusion, a proper attitude is the most important aspect of holiness. A person with a humble, teachable attitude and a genuine desire to live for God can always be led to greater truth. Inward holiness will lead to outward holiness, but the reverse is not true. We often forget this, because it is easy to observe and compare outward holiness but more difficult to discern inward holiness. Outward holiness is often the easiest part to obey, while attitudes and spirits are more difficult to control.

A wrong attitude can be just as sinful as an act that we commit. Let us check our hearts for pride, murmuring, sowing discord, bitterness, wrath, and other evil attitudes. It would be sad to live in outward conformity to scriptural teachings yet destroy our life of holiness through an evil attitude that we allow to creep into our heart.

CHAPTER

4

The Tongue: Unruly Member

But the tongue can no man tame; it is an unruly evil, full of deadly poison (James 3:8).

Let the words of my mouth . . . be acceptable in thy sight, O LORD (Psalm 19:14).

Unruly member. The tongue is the most difficult member of the body to control, and it has the potential for causing the most harm. The way we use the tongue is a good indication of our relationship with God. The tongue speaks whatever is in the heart. If we speak evil, then evil must be in our heart, "for out of the abundance of the heart the mouth speaketh" (Matthew 12:34). "Those things which proceed out of the mouth come forth from the heart; and they defile the man" (Matthew 15:18).

James contains strong teaching concerning the tongue. "If any man among you seem to be religious, and bridleth not his tongue, but deceiveth his own heart, this man's religion is vain" (James 1:26). "If any man offend not in word, the same is a perfect man, and able also to bridle the whole body" (James 3:2). The tongue is like a bit in a horse's mouth that controls the movements of the horse, a small helm that controls a large ship, and a small fire that can cause great trouble. The tongue can defile the whole body. Only the power of God can tame it (James 3:1-13).

The power of the tongue is apparently one reason why God has chosen speaking in tongues as the initial evidence of the Spirit baptism (Acts 2:4; 10:46; 19:6). We receive the Holy Spirit when we repent, believe, and surrender completely to God. Our tongue is the hardest member to tame, so it is the last part of us to yield to God. When we speak in tongues for the first time under the inspiration of the Spirit, it signifies that God has at last come inside and taken complete control.

James makes it clear that it is easy for us to sin with the tongue, that the tongue is dangerous, and that sinning with the tongue can destroy our holiness. Let us discuss some ways in which people sin with the tongue. Let us keep in mind that if it is wrong to speak some things, then it is wrong to listen to some things. Therefore, as we guard our tongue from evil, we should also guard our ear from evil, such as indulging in conversations or radio programs that are contrary to Christian values.

Talebearing or gossip is a vicious sin. It is Satan's primary tool for destroying the church from within. It can destroy confidence in people, harm the innocent, and hinder the repentant. It splits churches, discourages saints, and disillusions new converts. The Bible teaches us to speak evil of no one, especially our brothers and sisters in the Lord (Titus 3:2; James 4:11). "Whoso privily slandereth his neighbour, him will I cut off" (Psalm 101:5).

Most people will readily acknowledge the evils of talebearing, but the problem comes in identifying it in their own lives. It means telling things of a personal, intimate, or sensational nature that are harmful to someone. It involves damaging rumors and backbiting (speaking spitefully or slanderously about someone). Talebearing includes lying about someone or spreading negative rumors about someone, but it also includes telling facts of a personal, hurtful nature that the gossiper has no business revealing. Telling a fact can be talebearing when it is told as gossip to someone who does not need to know about it.

God has ordained organization and authority in the church (I Corinthians 12:28). (See chapter 12.) When problems arise in the church, those in authority should be informed. Leaders can and must judge situations in order to protect the flock (Matthew 18:18; I Corinthians 6:5).

However, needless disclosure to other members of the congregation is not right. Individuals are not to judge one another (Romans 14:10, 13; Matthew 7:1; James 4:12). Sometimes, information must be shared for clarification, instruction, or accuracy. In general, however, telling stories that could be harmful to others is not right in the sight of God. "Where no wood is, there the fire goeth out: so where there is no talebearer, the strife ceaseth. . . . The words of a talebearer are as wounds, and they go down into the innermost parts of the belly" (Proverbs 26:20, 22). How many churches would have peace if their members really believed this teaching of Scripture!

As a practical example, what should we do if we discover that a certain man in the church has committed adultery? We should not conceal the sin, for we do not have that authority. We should report the problem to someone in authority, such as the pastor, presbyter, or superintendent, depending on the person involved. At that point, the matter becomes the leader's responsibility. The reason is so that the leader can help the sinning brother and also protect others in the church who may be affected by the sin. If we cover up the sin, we could cause great damage to individuals, families, and the whole body.

There is no reason to tell others about the sin, however. If we tell everyone else in the church we become a talebearer. If the brother has repented, why tell others about the sin? How will it help him if we tell everyone else of his fall? The problem is a private matter to be handled by the person, those in authority over him, and the Lord.

As another example, suppose a person falls into sin, repents, and moves to another church. The former pastor should inform the new pastor so that the latter may help the person, but it is generally not appropriate or necessary to tell the other church members about the problem.

The foregoing examples are applications of Scripture. "A talebearer revealeth secrets: but he that is of a faithful spirit concealeth the matter" (Proverbs 11:13). "He that covereth a transgression seeketh love; but he that repeateth a matter separateth very friends" (Proverbs 17:9).

We do not have the authority to cover up unrepented sin, regardless of whether a friend is involved or not. Nor should we cover up sin that would scripturally disqualify a person from holding a position. In both cases, the person in authority needs to know. At the same time, we do not need to tell a friend's sin to others.

A private sin becomes a church problem when the person does not repent but lives as a hypocrite or when the person brings disgrace and reproach upon the church. This point is especially relevant when someone in a position of leadership has sinned. For example, what if a deacon in the church commits adultery but repents? The pastor should be informed because it is a matter that could disgrace the whole church and because the deacon has lost the necessary qualifications, namely, a good report. The one with whom the deacon has sinned as well as anyone else who finds out about the sin will lose confidence in the church if nothing is done. This does not mean that the pastor should make a public announcement of the repented sin. The pastor can relieve the person of spiritual responsibilities without any explanation except that it was by mutual agreement.

In other situations, the pastor may put people on probation or silence them for a period of time. Of course, people should not speculate or gossip about what has happened. It may be best for wrongdoers simply to explain that they need to take some time for personal refreshing, renewing, and refocusing. Sometimes this is beneficial even when no sin has been committed, so the congregation should expect such occurrences without undue suspicion.

What should we do if we hear that someone has said or done something against us? First, since love thinks no evil, we should not be quick to believe the rumor. Instead, we should give the person the benefit of doubt and assume that the story is erroneous or that there is a good explanation. Then we should forget about the report.

Second, if the report still bothers us, we should pray for the Lord to give us peace. If the matter cannot be dismissed easily, then we should pray for the Lord to resolve the problem.

Third, if the problem persists even after prayer, we should go to the person who is involved, get the story straight from him or her, and clear up the problem (Matthew 18:15).

What should we do if we hear about serious wrongdoing on the part of someone else? We should take the first two steps just mentioned of not being quick to believe the rumor and praying about the situation. If the situation cannot be ignored, then we should report the matter to those in authority—typically, the pastor.

It then becomes the pastor's responsibility to deal with the situation. The pastor can speak to the individual as needed. If the pastor is convinced that the rumor is false, then he or she should advise those who heard it. If there is significant reason to believe that the story is true, then the pastor has a duty to deal with the situation. Either way, we should not pass along the story to other people.

If those in authority hear about a serious problem, they should go to the person who is allegedly involved and seek to clear up the matter. If leaders ask us to explain a matter involving us, we should not become offended, because they are simply fulfilling their responsibility. They are giving us an opportunity to clear up a misunderstanding, and we need to keep a good spirit in this situation. There is no need to find out who started the rumor or who told the leaders, because this could easily lead to vengeance and malice. It is the leaders' job to clear up the matter and, in the case of a false report, to rebuke or correct those who perpetuated the story. If we are indeed innocent, we should appreciate it when someone reports the situation to the pastor instead of repeating it to others.

Sowing discord. The subject of talebearing is important because it is a principal means of sowing discord among believers. Sowing discord is one of seven abominations in Proverbs 6:16-19. An abomination is something God hates, and those who commit abominations will not go to heaven (Revelation 21:8).

To sow discord means to cause dislike, distrust, and division, and it often occurs by talebearing or constant criticism. Those who sow discord think they can tell anything anywhere, anytime, to anyone. They repeat information they heard in confidence and obtained through friendship. They are not afraid to criticize anyone.

We need to examine ourselves in this area. Do we enjoy gossiping about people? Do we spread negative or injurious information about others instead of talking to them directly about our concerns? Do we enjoy hearing something bad about someone? Do we enjoy telling everything we know? Do we enjoy criticizing or laying blame on others? Do we stir up trouble, dissension, and strife? If any of these things is true, we need to change our ways. It does not matter how well we can preach or sing, if we sow discord we are in trouble with God.

Swearing. "But above all things, my brethren, swear not, neither by heaven, neither by the earth, neither by any other oath . . . lest ye fall into condemnation" (James 5:12). Jesus said, "Swear not at all" (Matthew 5:34).

To swear means to assert something as true or promise something while under oath. An oath is a formal calling of God as a witness. The Bible teaches that we should not swear to anything or bind ourselves by an oath to do a certain thing or to join a certain group. Jesus explained that the law of Moses allowed people to swear by the Lord, but He instructed that under the new covenant we should not swear by anything—not by heaven (i.e., God), earth, or even by our own heads. The reason is that we do not have the power to change any of these things, to enforce our oaths, or to guarantee our promises. (See Matthew 5:33-37.) God can swear by Himself because He has the power to make whatever He says come to pass. If something did not exist before, it becomes true the minute He speaks it.

When we are called upon by law to swear to something, we can simply say, "I affirm." To affirm means to state positively, to confirm, or to assert as valid. As human beings we do not have the power to swear by oath, but we can affirm that what we are saying is true. As Christians our word should always be true, and our promise should be just as good as any oath. We should have only one standard of truth. We do not need to use the words "I swear" to prove that at least we are telling the truth this one time, for people should always be able to depend on our word. We do not swear because we cannot control the things we would swear upon, but we can make sure that we always tell the truth and that we perform our promises to the best of our ability.

Taking God's name in vain. "Thou shalt not take the name of the LORD thy God in vain" (Exodus 20:7). The commandments applicable today can be grouped into two categories: loving God and loving our neighbor

(Mark 12:28-31). This commandment pertains to loving God. It teaches us the proper use of His name. It prohibits all profane, meaningless, trivial, or irreverent use of God's name. It also covers any abuse of His name in false oaths, false religions, and witchcraft. The right way to use God's name is in praise, worship, preaching, teaching, prayer, and meditation. There is a blessing for those who think upon His name (Malachi 3:16).

The Jews were so careful about taking the name of the Lord in vain that they developed the custom of never pronouncing the name Jehovah or Yahweh. When reading aloud from the Hebrew Scriptures they would substitute the word *Adonai*, meaning Lord, for the sacred name Yahweh. When quoting or writing their Scriptures in Greek, they would use the Greek word *kurios*, which also means Lord. The writers of the New Testament followed this practice and so did the King James translators. For example, Isaiah 40:3 uses the Hebrew word Yahweh, which the translators represented by "LORD" (large and small capital letters). When Matthew quoted this verse in Greek, he used *kurios* (Matthew 3:3).

Unfortunately, many Christians treat God's name and titles casually. Often they will use the words *God*, *Lord*, *Jesus*, or *hallelujah* (which means "praise the Lord" in Hebrew) in a useless or lighthearted way. For many, it becomes a habit to use one of these words as a mere byword when they are happy, angry, sad, disappointed, or surprised. But we should only use these words when we are sincerely invoking God's help, communicating with Him, or talking about Him. If we use these words casually and thoughtlessly, then we diminish their value to inspire faith when we invoke them in prayer and praise. When we reserve these words for sincere, meaningful communication, then we show proper respect for God and preserve their value to inspire faith in the hearts of both speakers and hearers.

Slang. We should also be cautious when using slang expressions. Many slang words have negative connotations, and we can easily pick up a slang expression without realizing what it really means. What about watered down versions of curse words? If we do not want to use certain words, why use their derivatives and substitutes?

Filthy communication. "Put off . . . filthy communication out of your mouth" (Colossians 3:8). "Let no corrupt communication proceed out of your mouth" (Ephesians 4:29). We are the temple of the Holy Spirit, and as such we must not allow dirty jokes, words, and actions to come from us. Words that suggest something indecent should not come from the lips of a Christian. Should praises and vile words come out of the same mouth? "Doth a fountain send forth at the same place sweet water and bitter? Can the fig tree, my brethren, bear olive berries? either a vine, figs? so can no fountain both yield salt water and fresh" (James 3:11-12).

We are to have "neither filthiness, nor foolish talking, nor jesting" (Ephesians 5:4). This passage does not forbid entertainment, joking, or humor, but it tells us that holiness guidelines apply even in these activities. "Foolish talking" means idle, stupid talk. "Jesting" comes from the Greek word *eutrapelia*, which means "witticism, i.e. (in a vulgar sense) ribaldry."[1] It refers to coarse, obscene jesting. In other words, Christians should not take part in smutty, insinuating, sexually oriented stories, jokes, or actions. It is a shame even to talk about some things that are done in secret (Ephesians 5:12). Some things may be appropriate to discuss in a proper setting but not in public or in mixed company. Some things should be kept in confidence between husband and wife.

Cursing. "Bless them which persecute you: bless, and curse not" (Romans 12:14). "Out of the same mouth proceedeth blessing and cursing. My brethren, these things ought not so to be" (James 3:10). These verses deal with the practice of pronouncing a curse upon someone. The Christian attitude is not to return evil for evil but to overcome evil with good (Romans 12:21). Jesus commanded, "Love your enemies, bless them that curse you, do good to them that hate you, and pray for them which despitefully use you, and persecute you" (Matthew 5:44).

Some ministers misunderstand their authority and abuse their position by pronouncing curses upon people. In one case, a woman and her family did something the pastor did not like. In retaliation, he verbally pronounced a curse upon her. As we have just seen, this practice is contrary to the Word of God. All genuine exercise of spiritual gifts must take place with love and for edification. (See I Corinthians 13:1-3; 14:3.)

Sometimes, people cite biblical examples to justify cursing. Let us examine the three primary examples they use: II Kings 2:23-24; Acts 5:3-10; and Acts 13:10-11.

In II Kings 2, a group of young men from the city of Bethel mocked the prophet Elisha. They called him a "bald head," an epithet of contempt and derision in the Old Testament that meant "worthless fellow." They taunted him, "Go up," that is, "Be translated as you say your master, Elijah, was." Elisha rebuked them in the name of the Lord. Later two bears came out and tore forty-two of them.

This incident occurred under the old covenant, not in the context of New Testament ministry. We should also note that these men were already under divine condemnation. They were from Bethel, one of the two cities in the northern kingdom of Israel that had erected golden calves to worship (I Kings 12:29), and they were mocking the prophet of God and the power of God. Under the law, these men were already condemned to die because of their idolatry (Deuteronomy 13:12-15). God had already cursed them, and the question was simply when the judgment would be carried out. Because God does not always execute judgment speedily, people are prone to think that God has overlooked their sin (Ecclesiastes 8:11). In this case, God delayed His judgment until they began mocking His prophet. Elisha did not place them under a curse but pronounced that the time of God's judgment had come.

Acts 5 relates the story of Ananias and Sapphira. This couple tried to deceive the church by making a covenant to lie. God gave Peter a word of knowledge and revealed the truth to him. Peter did not personally curse Ananias and Sapphira but simply told Ananias that he was lying, whereupon God struck him dead. A short time later, God gave Peter another word of knowledge, and he prophesied that Sapphira would die just as her husband had.

When the law was first given, Aaron's disobedient sons suffered the penalty of death as an example to everyone of the importance of keeping God's Word (Leviticus 10:1-2). Similarly, Ananias and Sapphira died for their hypocrisy at the beginning of the New Testament church. Although hypocrites in the church do not generally die immediately, this example serves as a warning under the new covenant. In neither case did humans curse the offenders, however.

The last case concerns Paul and the sorcerer Barjesus, who opposed the preaching of the gospel in Cyprus. In this case, God gave Paul a word of knowledge as to what He was going to do, and Paul revealed it to Barjesus through prophecy. Paul said, "The hand of the Lord is upon thee, and thou shalt be blind" (Acts 13:11). Paul did not exhibit hatred or revenge, but this incident confirmed the truth of his message.

These examples do not give us the authority to curse other people, but they demonstrate the judgment of God upon sin. To curse someone would be in direct opposition to the Word of God. When people do something wrong, our attitude should be one of mercy and forgiveness. We should pray in love, "God, have mercy on them. Help them to understand their mistake, and lead them to repentance."

Reviling. "Nor revilers . . . shall inherit the kingdom of God" (I Corinthians 6:10). "But now I have written unto you not to keep company, if any man that is called a brother be . . . a railer, . . . with such an one no not to eat" (I Corinthians 5:11). To revile or to rail means to abuse using words; to use harsh, insolent, or abusive language.

Since we are the temple of the Holy Spirit, we should not follow fleshly emotions but respond according to the Spirit. Even if we have been mistreated or misjudged, we should not revile other people. In I Corinthians 4:12-13 we find the proper reaction when others revile us. The apostles were reviled, persecuted, defamed, and made as the filth of the world. Their response was to bless.

Paul was rebuked for reviling the high priest while

under questioning by the Sanhedrin council (Acts 23:1-5). Ananias, the priest, had commanded someone to slap Paul, which was contrary to the law. At the same time he was trying to judge Paul by the law. Paul quickly told Ananias that he was a "whited wall," or hypocrite, for doing this. When Paul said that, those standing by rebuked him for reviling God's high priest. When Paul realized that Ananias was the high priest, he apologized. He quoted Exodus 22:28, which prohibits the reviling of a ruler, and explained that he did not know he was speaking to the high priest when he said what he did. Either Paul did not know to whom he was speaking or he did not acknowledge the man's usurpation of office. In fact, according to history, Ananias usurped this office from which he had previously been expelled by the Romans for crimes. Paul recognized that even though he was being unjustly condemned, he should not revile the high priest, because of his office.

Even Michael the archangel did not bring a railing or reviling accusation against the devil when contending with him but simply said, "The Lord rebuke thee" (Jude 9). Michael did not abuse even Satan with words, remembering no doubt that Satan originally had been created as an anointed cherub. Jude contrasted Michael's good attitude with that of apostates who despise authority, speak evil of dignitaries, and speak evil of things they do not know (verses 8, 10).

Peter similarly described apostates, those who have forsaken truth to the point that they do not fear the Word of God. "But chiefly them that walk after the flesh in the lust of uncleanness, and despise government. Presumptuous are they, self-willed, they are not afraid to speak evil of dignities. Whereas angels, which are greater in power and might, bring not railing accusation against them before the Lord" (II Peter 2:10-11). These people do not want anyone to tell them what to do. They will not accept correction. They are not afraid to speak evil about those in authority over them. The fear of the Lord is the beginning of wisdom (Proverbs 9:10), but they have no fear or reverence for the Lord, His Word, His church, or His appointed leaders.

According to Peter and Jude, these people need to learn from the angels. The angels who have the responsibility to report to God about these same apostates do not rashly accuse or bitterly condemn them. They merely report the facts as they are without reviling or railing. They are courteous in their reports, even though they have more power than human beings.

Thus, we find that the apostles, including Paul, and the angels, including Michael, knew better than to revile. Yet many people do not hesitate to speak harshly to and about fellow believers, including leaders. Sometimes, believers speak disparagingly of their pastors, and ministers speak disparagingly about other ministers. Even if someone has sinned, however, there is a process by which to bring the matter before the proper authority. To report facts to those in authority is right, but to speak maliciously and to revile when reporting is wrong.

Jesus warned us to be careful of calling anyone a fool (Matthew 5:22). In the biblical context, this word connotes someone who is morally obstinate, not merely ignorant or simple. (See Psalm 14:1.) Thus, it represents strong condemnation and could become a means of reviling others.

Holiness teaches us not to speak evil about anyone

and not to revile anyone. Even if people have sunk to the depths of sin, we should not revile them. We should be especially careful not to revile leaders. Those who revile are doing something that the apostles and the angels refused to do, even with regard to the worst sinners and the devil himself.

Lying and bearing false witness. "Thou shalt not bear false witness against thy neighbor" (Exodus 20:16; Mark 10:19). "All liars, shall have their part in the lake which burneth with fire and brimstone" (Revelation 21:8). These verses and many others show us that God hates lies. Nothing that makes a lie, whether by speech or action, will enter into the New Jerusalem (Revelation 21:27). Two of the seven abominations (things God hates) in Proverbs 6:16-19 are a lying tongue and a false witness that speaks lies. Moreover, God wants us to keep our promises even if they hurt us (Psalm 15:4). In short, "he that speaketh lies shall not escape" (Proverbs 19:5).

To lie means to make a statement knowing that it is false, to say something with the intent to deceive. It can also involve deliberately giving a false impression to someone who has a right and expectation to know the full truth. In certain situations, it can even be dishonest to tell part of the truth—for example, if the effect is to conceal additional truth that is necessary to understand a situation correctly from someone who has a right to know. For this reason, we are to tell the truth, the whole truth, and nothing but the truth in a court of law.

A lie is a lie even if told for a good purpose. The end does not justify the means. For instance, suppose two people have an argument and refuse to speak to each other. A third person decides to be a mediator and falsely tells each person that the other has already apologized. Even though the purpose is to bring reconciliation, the third person has told a lie.

Suppose a teenager has parents who will not let him attend church. Should he lie about where he is going in order to attend? No, he should not commit sin in order to go to church. Suppose a woman is married to an unbelieving husband, and he forbids her to pay tithes on his income. She promises not to do so, but should she secretly give this money to the church anyway? No, she has given her word, and she would be lying if she broke it. She would defraud her husband and destroy his confidence in her.

Some cite the story of Rahab to demonstrate that the end justifies the means, because she lied to the people of Jericho in order to conceal Israelite spies. However, she was a Gentile who did not know the law of God. She heard about the great things Jehovah had done for Israel, and she believed in Him. As a result, she hid the spies and assisted them in their mission. She was not saved by lying but by her faith as demonstrated by works. God wanted to show His power through Israel so that all nations would see it, believe on Him, and be saved. Rahab was one person who obeyed this plan. If she had known God's law and had prayed accordingly, God could have made another way to deliver the spies. Moreover, this example involves concealment in order to save human life, and thus it would not justify lying in lesser circumstances.

Abraham lied on two occasions by saying that his wife, Sarah, was only his sister (Genesis 12:10-20; 20:1-16). He did this because he feared that foreign kings would kill him in order to marry Sarah, who was very beautiful. Sarah actually was Abraham's half sister, but he was dishonest in not telling these potential suitors that she was also his wife. Both times his deception almost led to disaster, since the kings tried to take Sarah as their wife, thinking she was available. Only the intervention of God restored her to Abraham. Abraham was reproved for his deception both times and was even expelled from the land one time. These incidents show that lying is wrong even when the purpose is to protect our legitimate interests, that lying causes more problems than it solves, that God can deliver us from difficult situations without our resorting to lies, and that telling a half-truth in order to create a false impression can be a lie.

On the other hand, we are not necessarily obligated to disclose everything we know about a situation, especially to someone who does not have a right to know this private information. In order to protect Samuel from the potential wrath of King Saul when Samuel went to anoint David as the future king of Israel, God told him to go to Bethlehem to offer a sacrifice. If someone were to inquire about his trip, he could honestly say that he was offering a sacrifice; he would not need to volunteer that he was also on a secret mission to anoint David. (See I Samuel 16:1-5.)

It is possible to "make a lie" by actions as well as words. What if a minister displays a false graduation diploma as if he had earned it? He is lying by giving a false impression. What if an office worker submits a receipt for reimbursement but actually the expense was less than the receipt shows? She has lied and committed fraud. Similarly, what if a worker requisitions money for one thing but spends it on something else? He has lied, unless he obtains authorization for the change. What if he does not spend the full amount of the requisition but pockets the difference? He has lied and committed fraud.

As Christians we do not have to lie. If we have not done anything wrong, we can trust God to help us and protect us in difficult situations. From an eternal perspective the old saying is true: Honesty is the best policy. (See chapter 11 for further discussion of honesty, integrity, and fraud.)

Careless words. Jesus said, "Out of the abundance of the heart the mouth speaketh. . . . Every idle word that men shall speak, they shall give account thereof in the day of judgment. For by thy words thou shalt be justified, and by thy words thou shalt be condemned" (Matthew 12:34, 36-37). If we speak carelessly, we could easily commit sin and could easily harm others. Therefore, we should think before we speak. What we talk about reveals what is in our heart, and what is in our heart determines whether we are living by faith in Jesus Christ.

Importance of the tongue. These words of Jesus demonstrate how important our speech is. As we noted at the beginning of this chapter, James 1:26 warns, "If any man among you seem to be religious, and bridleth not his tongue, but deceiveth his own heart, this man's religion is vain." On the other hand, "if any man offend not in word, the same is a perfect man, and able also to bridle the whole body" (James 3:2). In short, we need to have "sound speech, that cannot be condemned" (Titus 2:8). "Let your speech be alway with grace, seasoned with salt, that ye may know how ye ought to answer every man" (Colossians 4:6).

Ultimately, only God can help us control our tongues, so we must pray for His guidance and grace in this matter. "Let the words of my mouth . . . be acceptable in thy sight,

O LORD" (Psalm 19:14). "Set a watch, O LORD, before my mouth; keep the door of my lips" (Psalm 141:3).

Note

[1]James Strong, *Exhaustive Concordance of the Bible* (Nashville: Abingdon, 1890).

CHAPTER

5

The Eye: Light of the Body

The light of the body is the eye. . . . If thine eye be evil, thy whole body shall be full of darkness (Matthew 6:22-23).

I will set no wicked thing before mine eyes (Psalm 101:3).

Gate of the soul. David made a covenant with his eyes when he promised not to place any wicked thing in front of them. He also asked God to "turn away mine eyes from beholding vanity" (Psalm 119:37). Vanity refers to anything that is worthless, foolish, empty, and destitute of reality. Why did David place such emphasis on keeping his eyes free from beholding wicked and vain things?

The reason is that the eye is a unique member of the body in certain important respects. Jesus told us that the eye is the light of the body (Matthew 6:22-23; Luke 11:34). If it is "single" (clear, whole, not blinded), then the whole body will be full of light. If it is "evil" (wicked, diseased, blind), then the whole body will be full of darkness. If the light of the body is dark, how great is the darkness of the rest of the body! In other words, Jesus taught that the eye is the gate to the heart or soul. It is the principal sensory organ that we use to receive information from the outside world. If our eye is constantly filled with evil sights, then our thoughts and actions will be drastically affected.

Psychologists have verified this statement, estimating that 90 percent of our thought life is stimulated by what we see. Experiments have shown that the human brain retains in long-term memory about 65 percent of what it receives through the eyes and ears simultaneously but only about 15 percent of what comes through the ears alone. As a simple illustration of the impact of the eyes on the mind, we can think of the difference between seeing a horrible accident as opposed to merely hearing about it. There is much truth in the old saying, "Seeing is believing."

What we see has a powerful influence on our thoughts. In turn, our thoughts determine what kind of people we are. "For as he thinketh in his heart, so is he" (Proverbs 23:7). As Jesus said, the condition of the eyes determines the condition of the body as a whole. What the eyes indulge in and enjoy is what the body will indulge in and enjoy. For this reason, the "lust of the eyes" is one of the three major areas of worldliness and temptation (I John 2:16). While we can be tempted through other senses, the Bible does not speak of the lust of the nose or ears, because their influence is not nearly as significant as that of the eyes.

Temptation is the first step toward sin, and after lust

has conceived it brings forth sin (James 1:14-15). Often, temptation comes through the eyes. Eve saw that the forbidden fruit was pleasant to the eye, so she took it (Genesis 3:6). Achan saw a garment, some silver, and some gold. God had forbidden the Israelites from taking anything from Jericho, and no doubt Achan intended to obey, but when he actually saw these objects he explained, "Then I coveted them" (Joshua 7:21). David "saw a woman washing herself; and the woman was very beautiful to look upon" (II Samuel 11:2). This temptation led directly to adultery and eventually murder. Satan showed Jesus the kingdoms of the world from a mountaintop in order to tempt Him (Matthew 4:8). All these incidents show how powerful the eyes can be.

Satan knows that he can easily reach the mind through the eye. He tries to bring temptations before our eyes for several reasons. First, in this way we encounter suggestions that we had not previously known about or considered. Second, scenes can become embedded in our memories so that they are available to tempt us later when we are weak or discouraged. Third, constant exposure to certain sights and their associated ideas causes us gradually to become accustomed to them. We may eventually come to accept them as permissible, normal, or inevitable. Finally, if we think about certain things long enough, we will eventually sin—whether by entertaining and dwelling on these scenes in our minds or by committing a outward act of sin.

We must guard our eyes from temptations. Of course, many situations present themselves to us and yet we may have little control over them. For example, we may see immodest dress almost anywhere today. What should we as Christians do in this kind of situation? We may not be able to avoid such sights completely, but we can discipline our eyes and minds. We must not entertain, fantasize about, or deliberately prolong the temptation; for doing so can lead to sin, either in our minds or in our actions.

Important passages of Scripture. There are areas in modern society where we are able to exercise complete control over what we allow our eyes to see; namely, the use of visual media, including printed materials, television, movies, videos, CDs, DVDs, and the Internet. Let us look at some passages of Scripture that apply to our use of these media.

As we have discussed, evil can easily enter our minds through our eyes. Thus, whatever we are supposed to keep out of our minds, we should keep away from our eyes. Jesus said, "For out of the heart proceed evil thoughts, murders, adulteries, fornications, thefts, false witness, blasphemies: these are the things which defile a man" (Matthew 15:19-20). Isaiah 33:15-16 gives this promise: he "that stoppeth his ears from hearing of blood, and shutteth his eyes from seeing evil; he shall dwell on high."

Paul commanded, "Abstain from all appearance of evil" (I Thessalonians 5:22). After listing twenty-three sins of debased people, he further described them as follows: "who knowing the judgment of God, that they which commit such things are worthy of death, not only do the same, but have pleasure in them that do them" (Romans 1:32). Not only is it wrong to commit evil, but it is also wrong to take pleasure in others who commit evil. Thus, we should not entertain ourselves by the depiction and glorification of evil deeds. When we do, we think defiling thoughts. How can we take pleasure in the sins of others and yet fulfill the commandment, "Ye that love the LORD, hate evil" (Psalm 97:10)? As the psalmist prayed, "Let the words of my mouth, and the meditation of my heart, be acceptable in thy sight, O LORD" (Psalm 19:14).

Reading. Reading is one of the best means of self-education. Someone who loves to read will probably have a large vocabulary, good grammar, and a general knowledge of a variety of topics. Reading helps to keep the mind active. It can be a valuable source for intelligent conversation, preaching, and teaching. A well-read minister can refer and relate to contemporary issues in a useful way. There are many good books and magazines, both fiction and nonfiction.

At the same time, some reading material is not suitable for Christians. Examples are novels that glorify immorality or violence, explicit and graphic descriptions of sex, books filled with obscene and blasphemous words, pornographic magazines, magazines that focus on intimate confessions and scandals, and books that deal with witchcraft and the occult. If we feed on this type of material, then we will not have clean hearts. We must put away such books from our lives and destroy those in our possession, as did the church in Ephesus (Acts 19:19). If we read certain descriptions and absorb certain scenes, we plant them in our heart, and eventually they will proceed out of the heart.

If in doubt about whether to read something or not, we can ask: Are these meditations acceptable in the sight of God? The Holy Spirit will guide us in specific situations. Let us be sensitive to the Spirit and to the impressions He gives. We also have the laws of God written upon our hearts by faith, so our conscience, as informed by Scripture, can be a helpful guide. When we begin to read something that is unwholesome, the Holy Spirit can impress us not to continue. If we continue, our conscience will bother us. At that point, we have power either to suppress the voice of conscience or to obey it and do God's will.

Some say that novels are frivolous and unwholesome, but the reading of fiction can be a valid form of recreation and refreshment. Moreover, good fiction can stimulate thought, impart information, and increase language skills. Some types of fiction, such as comic books, may have little or no informative or educational value. It is advisable to limit the reading of this type of material and for parents to monitor and control its use.

Viewing. Technology has created many forms of visual media, including television, movies, videos, video games, CDs, DVDs, and the Internet. These media are a major area of concern in our day with respect to the lust of the eyes. As Christians, we should carefully regulate all use of media. While entertainment is not wrong, we must exercise great care when seeking entertainment in modern culture.

In making these decisions, we seek to implement the teachings of Psalm 101:2-3: "I will behave myself wisely in a perfect way. O when wilt thou come unto me? I will walk within my house with a perfect heart. I will set no wicked thing before mine eyes: I hate the work of them that turn aside; it shall not cleave to me." While we cannot prevent all temptations from coming to us, we should exercise control in areas of our own responsibility, especially the home. We also seek to follow Romans 1:32, which teaches that people who take pleasure in watching others commit sin are guilty of sin as well.

Technology is rapidly changing, leading to a proliferation of new choices and a merging with old choices. Thus, each generation needs to evaluate the situation in its day in order to make responsible Christian choices.

Since the vast majority of commercial TV programming is unwholesome and unproductive, we have chosen not to own a television. Likewise, since the vast majority of commercial movies are unwholesome, we have chosen not to attend theaters that feature Hollywood movies. We do not want to establish a habit that could harm our Christian witness, and we want to maintain a clear barrier against unnecessary temptation. The scope of the problem becomes clear when we realize that only about 3 percent of Hollywood movies are rated G (general audiences), while two-thirds are rated R (restricted).[1]

With regard to video, video games, CDs, DVDs, computers, and the Internet, we recognize that there is greater ability to make and regulate choices, so that people can choose to watch things that are wholesome, beneficial, inspirational, or educational. However, whatever is objectionable to watch on television or in movie theaters is objectionable to watch using these media. In all use of technology, we should only allow ourselves to view things that are consistent with family and Christian values. We also need to consider and follow the admonition of our pastor in this area. In all cases, parents should communicate clear guidelines to their children and personally monitor their viewing activities. Some good questions to ask are: Would I be comfortable showing this at church? Would I be willing to invite the pastor to watch with me?

For Internet use, we recommend placing the computer in a common area where its use can easily be seen by others and using a filtering program to block unwholesome sites. As a safeguard, parents should be able to monitor children's use, and spouses should be able to monitor spouses' use. It is wise for parents to instruct children to obtain their permission whenever they wish to use the Internet.

In selecting various visual media, we should carefully research their appropriateness for Christian viewing. Filtering guards can eliminate the occasional, unexpected use of inappropriate language. Detailed reviews are available online to assist in making wise decisions. Appropriate versions can also be purchased online from Christian or family-oriented companies.

In making choices, however, we cannot rely completely on the rating systems of the world or even the reviews of denominational Christians. For instance, a G-rated DVD may feature people who are immodestly and provocatively dressed, such as in a beach scene, or the plot may promote immorality. Content formerly deemed to warrant an R rating, which is clearly contrary to Christian values, is now often being rated as PG (parental guidance suggested) or PG-13 (parents strongly cautioned).[2] A study by the Harvard School of Public Health showed that the Motion Picture Association of America rating standards for sex and violence in movies have been getting weaker.[3] In general, we should *not* assume that a PG rating is consistent with family and Christian values.

On the other hand, an animated DVD based on the Book of Exodus was rated PG for mild violence merely because it depicted the Egyptian army drowning in the

Red Sea. A Christian-themed movie about a football coach's faith in God was rated PG allegedly for its religious content.[4]

For video games, we have instructed our children not to play anything that involves their killing of humans, that graphically depicts bloodshed, or that promotes immorality. We monitor both content and use of time. A rating of T (teen) indicates content that is potentially inappropriate, while M (mature) and A (adult) are clearly contrary to Christian values.

The problem with television, movies, and other media. First, the kinds of things displayed on the screen are generally not conducive to Christian living. Violence and sex are the two most common topics. Immodest clothing, assault, adultery, fornication, lying, hatred, cursing, drinking, smoking, filthy speech, and murder are among the evils shown almost constantly. This list sounds remarkably like the things in Matthew 15:19-20 that defile a person. Most of the programming consists of activities in which Christians should not participate. The scriptural admonitions, "I will set no wicked thing before mine eyes," "Abstain from all appearance of evil," and "Let the meditation of my heart be acceptable," are all applicable. How can we profess to hate evil if we indulge in watching these scenes? How can we avoid the condemnation of Romans 1:32 on those who take pleasure in watching others sin?

The viewer is bombarded with evil scenes and ungodly behavior. This evil goes directly from the eyes to the heart or mind. The result is to undermine resistance to sin. The mind is constantly tempted and encouraged to sin. By seeing sin repeated over and over, the mind gradually comes to the conclusion that it is not so bad after all. Viewers subconsciously assume that society in general is similar to what they see on the screen and that everyone else is living that way. The result is a compromising and permissive attitude.

As psychologists verify, television and movies are a form of escapism. The mind subconsciously identifies with the actors and plays their roles as a means of escaping the drudgery of life. Thus, the viewer's mind is polluted by participating vicariously in unwholesome scenes. In short, television and movies are a source of temptation and pollution of the heart or mind. They gradually erode defenses and alter attitudes toward sin through subtle influences. They entertain the carnal nature and feed the lusts of the flesh. Constant viewing of the standard fare of television and movies undermines spirituality.

Second, television is mostly a waste of time. Viewers are drawn to watch it hour after hour. However, it teaches almost nothing of value about real life, but it introduces artificial lifestyles and false values. Television has an allure and attraction, but long-term viewing wastes valuable time. In short, television can be a form of addiction. Habitual television viewing thus fits the definition of vanity—something useless, worthless, and destitute of reality. The prayer of David is relevant here: "Turn away mine eyes from beholding vanity" (Psalm 119:37).

In sum, television is dangerous because of the evils it displays and also because it robs people of valuable time. How many people have little or no time for prayer, Bible study, church services, or outreach but spend several hours a day in front of the television? How many people would spend the same amount of time in prayer as they do watching television? Christians neglect their walk with God, parents neglect their children, husbands and wives neglect each other, and students neglect their studies.

It is sad that the majority of American families now eat dinner in front of the TV instead of talking meaningfully with each other. The addictive and destructive power of TV is evident by the many nights it steals from quality family time. In many homes, the TV is left on almost all the time, even when entertaining guests. The admonition of Paul is particularly appropriate: "Redeeming the time, because the days are evil" (Ephesians 5:16). (See also Colossians 4:5.)

Television is particularly detrimental to children. By the time children start school, they have typically spent more time watching TV than they will spend in a college classroom. TV is often used as a babysitter, replacing opportunities for family interaction, imaginative play, and learning—all of which are vital for children.

The danger of using TV as a babysitter is evident when we consider that people's personality, morals, and values are formed primarily in early childhood. Television is the best way to introduce children to violence and lust. It encourages them to sin and to rebel against authority, and it suggests new ways of doing so. It leads them to believe that what they see on the screen is normal and typical. Even if parents think they are strong enough to completely ignore temptation (a faulty assumption), children definitely are not.

Medical doctors, psychologists, sociologists, and social commentators have researched the effects of television on the human mind, especially on the mind of children. The following sources report some of these findings and describe the power and danger of television from a secular point of view. Although the comments are directed primarily toward television, they apply to other visual media when used in the same manner.

Below is information from some of these sources. As we note the powerful influence of TV, we should keep in mind that most of the content is worldly, tempting, or even sinful. The combination of psychological power and spiritual harm makes TV a dangerous force indeed.

Michael and Diane Medved, *Saving Childhood.*[5] The authors are a Jewish couple; he is a radio talk show host and former film critic, while she is a psychologist in private practice. They describe how modern culture destroys the innocence of childhood, leading to much of the dysfunctional and destructive behaviors in society today. In response, parents need to protect their children from these assaults and provide children with security, a sense of wonder, and optimism (faith).

They particularly document the powerfully negative influence of television and movies, including television news. TV is on in the average home for 7.28 hours per day. The average person watches TV for 24 hours per week, or the equivalent of 10 uninterrupted *years* of life. Adults who complain about being too busy still watch TV for 10 hours a week. By age 5, a child will spend more time watching TV than talking to his or her father in a *lifetime*. The Medveds conclude: "Our strongest suggestion for maintaining your kids' sense of wonder is *cut out—or cut down on*—TV. . . . The problem is not too much sex or too much sleaze or too much violence, *it's too much TV—period.*" Their solution is as follows:

> The Medved family has never owned a TV. . . .

Upon proposing to Diane, Michael had one potentially deal-breaking stipulation: no TV. . . . We do own a video monitor, however, though absence of any antenna or cable makes TV reception impossible. We allow our three children to watch selected and approved videos that we own or rent, up to six hours a week.

Marie Winn, *The Plug-In Drug.*[6] Here are quotations with some added comments.

- "Even the most conservative estimates indicate that preschool children in America are spending more than one quarter of their waking hours watching television."
- Reporting on a study of a town that was the last one in an area to receive TV: "The findings were dramatic. Before television was introduced, the Notel children tested significantly higher than the kids in the other towns on tests of various skills. When re-tested a year after television's introduction, the Notel children's scores had gone down to the level of the kids in the other towns."
- "I suggest that the hyperactive child is attempting to recapture the dynamic quality of the television screen by rapidly changing his perceptual orientation." [The significant increase in the diagnosis of ADHD (attention deficit hyperactivity disorder) may well be linked to TV.]
- "One reason people talk about their television viewing so ruefully, so apologetically [is that] they are aware that it is an unproductive experience, that by human measure almost any other endeavor

is more worthwhile."

- "By the seventh edition of *Baby and Child Care*, published in 1998, Dr. Spock and his new co-author had begun to take a strongly negative view of television. 'Of all the media, television has the most pervasive influence on children,' a new section on television begins. Unequivocally stating that television viewing promotes passivity and 'requires zero mental activity on the viewer's part,' that 'watching TV is incompatible with creativity,' and going on to suggest that television viewing 'impairs children's ability to learn to read and fosters a short attention span,' Dr. Spock came up with a perfect solution to this serious problem: 'In my opinion, not having a TV at all seems to be a logical solution.'"
- "Evidence that the more television children view, the worse they do in school has been accumulating since research on television's impact on children began."
- "Children are known to spend 4,000 more hours watching television in the course of their school careers than they actually spend in the classroom."
- "Parents were firmer before the television era, . . . simply because firmness was necessary for parents' survival."
- "Through the change it has made in family life, television emerges as *the* important influence in children's lives today."
- "The most telling statistic: almost 60 percent of all families watch television during meals, and not necessarily at the same TV set."
- "What emerges from talks about television in the family is a picture of the parents' steady loss of

control as they gradually withdraw from an active role in the children's upbringing."

- "Television has undoubtedly had the deepest influence—not through the programs children watch, but indirectly, through the hours of steady, day-after-day, year-after-year socialization that television viewing has displaced."
- "When parents get to feel a connection of some kind with their children, they invariably begin to turn the television set off. Sometimes they even get rid of it."
- Quote from Colman McCarthy, a *Newsweek* columnist, after he eliminated TV from his home: "What had been happening all those years of watching television, I see now, was not only an addiction but also, on a deeper level, an adjustment. All of us had become adjusted to living with a stranger in the house. Is there any more basic definition of a television set than that?" [In this regard, Christians should ask, Would we allow strangers to come into our home to drink, smoke, curse, engage in violent behavior, and engage in immoral activity while we and our children watched them? If not, why allow them to do so via electronic media?]
- "Whatever the motivation for their televisionless state, the no-television-ever families interviewed for this book present a solid front: not a single parent or child among them expressed the desire to acquire a television set."
- "No-television-ever parents are often asked if they find the job of bringing up children much harder in the absence of a television set. But these parents

believe their life is easier, partly because their children are more resourceful, and partly because an area of conflict has been eliminated."

- "These televisionless families seem to spend considerably more time eating together than other families and their meals are characterized by more family conversation."
- "One aspect of television distinguishes it from all other past technologies that have affected society. No other advance had ever affected the lives of children under the age of six—the most impressionable segment of the population—as swiftly, pervasively, and directly as the coming of television to the American home."
- Quote from Robert Putnam, a Harvard social historian: "A major commitment to television viewing—such as most of us have come to have—is incompatible with a major commitment to community life." [As Christians, we would add: "and to church life."]

TV Turnoff Network.[7]

- Average number of hours per week that American one-year-old children watch television: 6. Number of hours recommended by the American Academy of Pediatrics for children two and under: 0.
- Average time per week that the American child ages 2-17 spends watching television: 19 hours, 40 minutes. Time per week that parents spend in meaningful conversation with their children: 38.5 minutes.
- Percentage of television time that children ages 2-7 spend watching alone and unsupervised: 81.

Percentage of television time that children older than 7 spend without their parents: 95.

- Percentage of children ages 8 and up who have no rules about watching TV: 61.
- Hours per year that the average American youth spends in school: 900. Hours per year that the average American youth watches television: 1,023.

American Academy of Pediatrics, *Television and the Family*.[8]

- "TV programs and commercials often show violence, alcohol or drug use, and sexual content that are not suitable for children or teenagers. Studies show that TV viewing may lead to more aggressive behavior, less physical activity, altered body image, and increased use of drugs and alcohol."
- The typical child "will have seen about 8,000 murders on TV by the time he finishes grade school. . . . Research also shows a very strong link between exposure to violent TV and violent and aggressive behavior in children and teenagers."
- "Television exposes children to adult behaviors, like sex. But it usually does not show the risks and results of sexual activity. On TV, sexual activity is shown as normal, fun, exciting, and without consequences. In commercials, sex is often used to sell products and services."
- "TV programs and commercials often show people who drink and smoke as healthy, energetic, sexy, and successful."
- "The average child sees more than 40,000 commercials each year."

Other research.

- In 2005, "a Kaiser Family Foundation study found that 77 percent of prime-time [television] shows contained sexual content, up from 67 percent in 1998. More than one in 10 shows overall featured 'scenes in which sexual intercourse is either depicted or strongly implied.' . . . Meantime, one-third of children 6 and under live in homes where the television is left on all or most of the time—whether or not anyone is watching. More than 40 percent of 4- to 6-year-olds have a television in their bedroom. For older children, that share is almost 70 percent."[9]
- "A recent study by the RAND Corporation and the University of California found that, for children ages 12 to 17, those who watched a lot of racy TV were twice as likely to start having sexual intercourse as those who watched very little."[10]
- Bhutan, a small Buddhist country between China and India, was the last nation in the world to introduce television, in 1999. People's behavior began to change, as children neglected homework, monks neglected their religious duties, and violence increased. Three years after TV's arrival, Bhutan experienced its first crime wave, including murder, fraud, and drug offenses. The national newspaper, *Kuensel*, blamed television: "We are seeing for the first time broken families, school dropouts and other negative youth crimes. We are beginning to see crime associated with drug users."[11]
- "According to the London School of Economics, . . .

> 90 percent of children will fall victim to pornography in their own homes," on the Internet.[12] Currently, there are over 4 million pornographic websites.

Other interesting sources are Jerry Mander, *Four Arguments for the* Elimination *of Television*, and Neil Postman, *Amusing Ourselves to Death.*[13]

Summary and response to objections. We have abundant evidence of the adverse spiritual, mental, emotional, and physical effects of television. It feeds the lusts of the flesh, is a constant source of temptation, is a thief of time, harms family life, warps children's character and morals, promotes sin, and is psychologically detrimental. Under these circumstances, Christians are better off without its influence. As technology continues to change and new options and new circumstances develop, Christians should carefully regulate all use of visual media in accordance with Christian values.

In view of current circumstances, a large body of Spirit-filled ministers has concluded that television as we know it today is not conducive to spiritual living. God has given ministers to the church for the perfecting of the saints and has given them power to bind and loose things in heaven and on earth. On such a crucial issue, we would do well to abide by the decision of the body.

Some respond that many programs are good, or at least not bad. As examples, people mention the news, documentaries, historical events, and cultural events. It is true that some programs on TV are not bad in themselves. Moreover, there is nothing wrong with the technology itself. However, even the news is often slanted and often glorifies violence, crime, and rebellion. The commercials often convey undesirable messages. Then, too, it is almost impossible to be sure that some ungodly scene or language will not come on an otherwise good program.

The main problem is that once people start watching TV they tend to look at just about anything that comes on, regardless of their good intentions. It is hard to turn off the TV in the middle of an unwholesome but interesting program. Viewers are inclined to justify themselves by making an exception, while TV's subtle influence is allowed to work. In theory, it is possible to choose only good things, but in practice it is difficult to exercise this degree of self-discipline. Since relatively few programs are wholesome and worthwhile, a Spirit-filled believer would have very little to watch and should not mind giving up TV for the sake of greater spirituality and unity. As technology develops in the direction of greater choice and greater control, we can take advantage of the ability to personalize our use of visual media in a way that is consistent with biblical teaching.

A second objection is that TV is not significantly worse than the temptations and worldliness to which we are exposed simply by living in our society. However, there is a difference between encountering sin in the world and inviting it into the sanctity of the home. It is like the difference between temptation entering the mind (which is not sin) and entertaining temptation until it becomes lust (which results in sin). The home is our place of security and safety. We may not be able to clean up the whole world, but we can try to keep our own house clean. After exposure to the sin of the world all day, it is important to come to a home where there is rest, peace, love, and holiness. Whatever we allow in our home, we endorse—

especially in the eyes of our children. It is one thing to recognize that sin exists, but it is another thing to endorse it, entertain it, flirt with it, and enjoy its display.

Conclusion. What is the position of Christians who habitually watch worldly programming on television and other media? Do they still hate evil? Apparently, their love is in the wrong place. This position is dangerous, for "if any man love the world, the love of the Father is not in him" (I John 2:15). If we bring television into the home, it will be difficult for us to mind the things of the Spirit and to maintain a close walk with God. Worldly programming will sap our power with God and subtly influence us in the wrong direction.

Since not all content is sinful, we cannot say that watching one program for one time is necessarily a sin, but even occasional viewing can be detrimental or dangerous. Because much of the content is sinful, frequent viewing is likely to lead to sin, for it is difficult to avoid all inappropriate content when it is so readily available. It is sinful to indulge in carnal lusts and to take pleasure in evil.

We should note the importance of following personal convictions in this area. Whatever is not of faith is sin (Romans 14:23), and a knowing failure to do what is good is sin (James 4:17). We should also heed the words of the wise man in Ecclesiastes 7:29: "God hath made man upright; but they have sought out many inventions."

Notes

[1]*USA Today*, 18 May 1997.

[2]*Christianity Today*, 16 June 1989.

[3]Sam Hananel, "Christian Movie's Rating Worries Lawmakers," Associated Press, 1 July 2006, online: news.yahoo.com.

[4]Ibid.

[5]Michael Medved and Diane Medved, Ph.D., *Saving Childhood: Protecting Our Children from the National Assault on Innocence* (New York: HarperCollins, 1998).

[6]Marie Winn, *The Plug-In Drug: Television, Computers and Family Life*, rev. ed. (New York: Penguin, 2002).

[7]TV Turnoff Network, online: www.tvturnoff.org, 21 April 2003.

[8]American Academy of Pediatrics, *Television and the Family* (Chicago: AAP, 2003), booklet.

[9]Ruth Marcus, "Concerned parents see popular culture going down the tube," *Austin American-Statesman*, 24 June 2006, A19.

[10]*Reader's Digest*, February 2005, 34.

[11]*London Guardian*, 14 June 2003; Public Broadcasting Service, *Frontline/World*, May 2002.

[12]Rebecca Hagelin, "Taking Back Our Homes," *Imprimis* (Hillsdale College), April 2006, 2.

[13]Jerry Mander, *Four Arguments for the* Elimination *of Television* (New York: Morrow, 1978); Neil Postman, *Amusing Ourselves to Death: Public Discourse in the Age of Show Business* (New York: Penguin, 1984).

CHAPTER

6

Scriptural Apparel and Adornment

In like manner also, that women adorn themselves in modest apparel, with shamefacedness and sobriety; not with broided hair, or gold, or pearls, or costly array (I Timothy 2:9).

The woman shall not wear that which pertaineth unto a man, neither shall a man put on a woman's garment: for all that do so are abomination unto the LORD thy God (Deuteronomy 22:5).

Outward appearance is an important aspect of holiness. The Bible teaches Christians how to dress and how to adorn themselves, giving principles that govern the outward appearance.

It is important to understand principles in this area for at least two reasons. First, styles of dress and customs have changed since the days of the Bible, so that we must apply its teachings to situations unknown in that day. Second, few statements in the New Testament specifically deal with men's appearance, since men's adornment was generally not a problem in those days. By identifying principles, we can apply the teaching to both men and women. Thus, in this chapter we discuss five scriptural principles for adornment and dress.

1. Modesty. Christians are to wear modest clothing (I Timothy 2:9). The Greek word for "modest" is *kosmios*, which means "orderly, well-arranged, decent, modest."[1] Here it describes someone who is decent or chaste, especially in outward dress and deportment. In explaining how women should adorn themselves, the apostle Peter explained that wives can win their unsaved husbands by their chaste conduct (I Peter 3:2). Modesty is particularly important when we appear in public in view of the opposite sex.

In the beginning, God created Adam and Eve in a state of innocence, and it seems that they were clothed with His glory. (See Genesis 2:25; Psalm 8:5.) Their relationship of physical, mental, and spiritual union was pure. When they sinned against God by eating fruit of the tree of knowledge of good and evil, they lost God's glory, realized that they were naked, and tried to clothe themselves with fig leaves. The pure relationship between man and woman was now capable of being distorted and polluted by sin, especially as the human race multiplied. Thus, God clothed Adam and Eve with animal skins to cover their nakedness (Genesis 3:21). Since that time, it has been His plan for humans to be decently clothed.

The devil tries to do just the opposite to humans. One of the things that the demon-possessed man of Gadara did was to take off his clothes. When Jesus cast out the demons, the man was found fully clothed and in his right mind (Luke 8:27, 35).

Immodest apparel can indicate the presence of a lustful spirit—a desire to flaunt the body and to attract the opposite sex by lust. Immodesty is a strong temptation and enticement, especially for men, who are more visually oriented and more easily aroused than women. David fell into adultery because of the lust of the eyes (II Samuel 11:2). It is easy for a man to sin in his heart by looking at an immodestly clothed woman (Matthew 5:28). In such a case the man is guilty, but the woman is not completely innocent either. God's plan for us today is to dress modestly.

Modest apparel means clothing that does not indecently expose the body to the opposite sex, whether intentionally or carelessly. In this regard, we should be mindful of sleeve length, necklines, dress length, tight clothes, and thin clothes. Both men and women need to develop a personal sense of modesty, wearing clothing that is appropriate to the occasion—whether sitting or standing, remaining still or praising God joyfully. For example, to implement the principle of modesty under various circumstances, we recommend that sleeves cover the upper arm and that dresses cover the knee.

2. Avoiding personal ornamentation. The word *modest* also has the connotation of not being showy or flashy. A woman should adorn herself with "shamefacedness and sobriety" and not with personal ornaments such as elaborately arranged hair (particularly braiding jewelry into the hair), gold, pearls, or extremely costly garments (I Timothy 2:9). "Shamefacedness" means reverence, self-restraint, modesty, and bashfulness. "Sobriety" means discretion, temperance, and self-control.

In short, Christians are not to dress in a vain way. God hates pride (see chapter 3), and He does not approve of a pretentious or ostentatious display. Styles that are primarily designed to feed the ego are not appropriate. Women should not rely on outward adorning to establish their identity. "Whose adorning let it not be that outward adorning of plaiting the hair, and of wearing of gold, or of putting on of apparel; but let it be the hidden man of the heart, in that which is not corruptible, even the ornament of a meek and quiet spirit, which is in the sight of God of great price" (I Peter 3:3-4).

It is acceptable to "adorn" oneself with "modest apparel." There is nothing wrong with ornamental aspects of clothing—such as colors, patterns, buttons, bows, scarves, and ties—as long as they remain in moderation. Clothing should be primarily functional and only secondarily ornamental. However, Scripture specifically instructs us not to adorn ourselves with precious stones and metals. This teaching forbids ornamental jewelry, whether real or imitation.

3. Moderation in cost. Closely associated with the avoidance of ornaments is the principle of moderation in cost. For this reason, we are not to adorn ourselves with gold, pearls, or "costly array." The definition of costly clothing may vary somewhat depending on the culture, society, and income of the individual. A good test is to ask if certain clothing would be an ostentatious display of wealth in the sight of acquaintances and fellow believers. Would it unduly arouse envy? Would it represent good stewardship of the money God has entrusted to our care? Surely it grieves God to see His people buying extravagant clothing, jewelry, and automobiles while they neglect His kingdom and His work suffers in many areas. God has blessed America materially, and He has blessed many Christians financially. He wants us to use our prosperity to support efforts to win the lost and to help the needy, not merely to satisfy our own desires.

4. Distinction between male and female. Deuteronomy 22:5 states another important concept to God—distinction between male and female. Not only are there biological differences between the sexes, but there are mental and emotional differences as well. In addition, God has established certain social methods for maintaining the distinction between male and female—namely, dress and hair length. (See chapter 7.) This separation is important to God because He has designed different roles in life for the male and the female. (See chapter 3.) In society, this distinction is an important guard against homosexuality, which God hates. (See chapter 9.) The principle of sex distinction in dress is violated by unisex clothing, by men dressing in a feminine way, and by women dressing in a masculine way.

Deuteronomy 22:5 applies today. Many argue that this Old Testament verse does not apply today. Some say that since both sexes wore robes in Bible days there was no clear distinction. While it is true that both wore robes, it is also true that there were clear differences in the types of robes worn by males and those worn by females. This fact is evident from a study of the history and culture of the Middle East as well as from the existence of this teaching in Deuteronomy.

Another objection is that Deuteronomy 22:5 is part of

the law given to Israel and does not concern us as Christians. For instance, today we do not literally obey verses 9-11, which prohibit mixing of seed when sowing, plowing with an ox and a donkey yoked together, and weaving wool and linen together in one garment.

To answer this objection, we must rightly divide the Word of God by looking at what these verses are intended to teach us. Verse 5 teaches the distinction of the sexes, which is a moral law. It was not instituted just for Israel, but it originated with creation and is still relevant today. Verses 9-11 teach the principle of separation, using physical objects as types of spiritual separation. Today, we do not obey the ceremonial aspects of the law as found in verses 9-11, but we do fulfill them in typology. Our separation today is not between kinds of seeds, animals, and fibers but between holy and unholy, spiritual and carnal.

We clearly see the difference in the two types of law, moral and ceremonial, in this chapter because verse 5 uses the word *abomination* but verses 9-11 do not. Specifically, verse 5 says that it is an "abomination unto the LORD thy God" for a person to wear clothes pertaining to the opposite sex. An abomination is something hated or detested, so verse 5 speaks of something that God hates.

God does not change in His likes and dislikes, for He has declared, "I am the LORD, I change not" (Malachi 3:6). God has "repented," or changed His mind, about whether to execute judgment, depending on people's repentance, but His basic character does not change. He is absolute in holiness and in His hatred of sin.

Thus, God's people of all ages must shun what is an abomination to Him. Christians do not need to keep the purely ceremonial part of the Jewish law, for it has been fulfilled in Jesus Christ. (See Colossians 2:16-17.) The ceremonial law did not relate to things God hated but to specific methods of worship and specific marks of identification. In some cases, God designated things as an abomination to Israel—that is, something the Israelites were supposed to hate—but refrained from calling them abominations to Him. As an example, God told Israel that certain animals were abominations to them and unclean to them (Leviticus 11). They were not called abominations to God or to us today. Wearing clothes of the opposite sex is an abomination to God, however, so it is an abomination to God's people of every age. In this connection, we should note that no abomination will enter the New Jerusalem but will be cast into the lake of fire (Revelation 21:8, 27).

New Testament teaching on distinction between male and female. The New Testament shows that God still considers distinction of the sexes to be important. According to I Corinthians 11, men should have short hair while women should have long hair. (See chapter 7.) According to I Corinthians 6:9-10, the "effeminate" will not inherit the kingdom of God. This passage uses two Greek words to describe homosexual activity. The one translated as "effeminate" is *malakos*, which has the connotation of being soft and effeminate. While the focus is on the sin of homosexuality, part of the problem is that some men act and dress like women.

Modern application of distinction in dress. Deuteronomy 22:5 covers all cultures. "That which pertaineth unto a man" means clothing traditionally associated with men or patterned after men's clothing. The type of clothing may vary with culture. For example, in Scotland the kilt was traditionally a man's garment, and in some parts of Asia and the Pacific, men wear similar garments. If a certain type of garment has been traditionally and culturally used exclusively by one sex and it is different from similar garments worn by the opposite sex, then it is permissible for the one sex to wear and not for the other sex.

In Western culture, the distinctive clothing of men is pants, and the distinctive clothing of women is dresses and skirts. Although cultural views are changing to allow certain unisex fashions, when Westerners emphasize masculine versus feminine dress they fall back on this distinction. For instance, the doors of public restrooms often have a silhouette of a man in pants and a woman in a dress. A book published by the Smithsonian Institution explains:

> In all times and places men and women have worn distinctively different clothing or adornment. . . . In cultures where trousers have become symbols of masculinity, women wearing trousers causes questions about women looking and acting like men. . . . In Western culture, trousers were associated with . . . masculinity since the Middle Ages. . . . Among the most powerful of these gender symbols in America have been skirts, trousers, and hair. Men have traditionally worn trousers, women skirts. . . . When members of one sex defied tradition by appropriating one of these symbols for themselves, the reaction was immediate. The Bloomer Costume in the 1850s and long hair [on men] in the 1960s are two of the most vivid examples of this phenomenon. Women bobbing their hair in the 1920s, women wearing trou-

sers to work in the 1970s, and men wearing skirts in the 1980s are others.[2]

The practice of women wearing pants did not gain widespread acceptance in America until World War II. At that time women began to take men's places in factories, as the men went off to war. Around this time, it also became widely accepted for women to cut their hair, smoke cigarettes, and drink alcoholic beverages. When society was disrupted and women assumed men's roles, then it became acceptable for women to wear pants—first for factory work, then for informal occasions, and finally for general public use, including office and church.

Today, most women wear pants sometimes, yet on formal occasions or occasions when they wish to accentuate their femininity, they usually wear dresses. Few men, however, will wear a dress. Indeed, most denominational Christians would disapprove of a man wearing a dress. For example, most would not accept a male pastor who wears a dress in the pulpit. Yet, from the scriptural viewpoint, both actions should be treated in a similar manner.

Although some pants are designed for women, typically they are closely patterned after men's clothing and would still fit under the definition of "that which pertaineth unto a man." "To pertain" means to belong to as a part, attribute, feature, or function; to have reference; to relate. In many cases, women wear styles that are exactly the same as men's styles, such as jeans, military fatigues, and sweat pants. When pants are designed for women, they can be quite formfitting and revealing, and if so they violate the principle of modesty.

5. Separation from the world. Another important principle of outward holiness is separation from the world. (See chapter 1.) God visibly separated the Israelites from the rest of the nations by their food, dress, farming practices, worship ceremonies, and Sabbath rest. It was usually possible to identify Jews simply by observing their dress and actions. As a result of their unique identity, the Jews have survived as the only ancient biblical people to maintain their cultural and religious heritage.

The Egyptians today do not have the same culture, religion, or language as in the days of the pharaohs. The Persians, Syrians, Greeks, and Romans do not have their ancient cultural, religious, and political systems. Most other tribes and nations that coexisted with Israel—such as the Hittites, Babylonians, Edomites, Assyrians, Philistines, and Ammonites—have not even survived as distinct nations. Yet the Jews have maintained their cultural identity through Babylonian captivity, Roman occupation, and nineteen hundred years without a homeland. The reason is that God's laws separated them from other nations and preserved their identity.

Similarly, for Christians to exist as a chosen people, they must have points of separation, both external and internal. In relation to dress and adornment, God has not given us arbitrary commands, but He has chosen points of distinction that also achieve His other objectives of modesty, moderation, humility, and sex differentiation. Consequently, Christian guidelines for conduct and dress help us to remain separate from the world around us. They help to distance us from temptation and sin, and they help us to maintain our identity.

Because of this principle of separation, Christians

sometimes avoid certain activities, hairstyles, and clothing that do not violate specific scriptural statements but nevertheless are closely associated with worldly attitudes and behavior. In another culture and time they might be permissible, but if they identify us with an ungodly lifestyle in our society then we avoid them. For instance, if a certain style of adornment or dress is closely associated with sexual promiscuity, homosexuality, or pagan religion, then Christians avoid it. As an example, the hippies of the 1960s used their hair and dress to express rebellion and sexual permissiveness, so Christians avoided looking like them. Similarly, the communist Chinese used unisex Mao suits as a symbol of their political and social views.

We must exercise caution in following the latest fads and fashions of the world. It is not wrong to follow fashions as long as they are consistent with biblical principles. However, we do not want to become closely identified with a worldly spirit, nor do we want to get caught up in a spirit of competition. Instead, we want to be examples of modesty, moderation, humility, and holiness.

Our dress should be appropriate to the occasion. Good taste and custom can guide us in this matter. When finances prohibit someone from being well dressed, there is certainly no question of holiness. We should not treat a poorly dressed person any different from a rich, well-dressed person, but we should be kind and accepting of both (James 2:1-9). Even in cases of poverty, however, Christians can strive to be clean and neat. We are ambassadors of Christ, so we should represent Him as well as possible.

In short, our outward appearance tells others much

about our lifestyle, beliefs, and attitudes. We should ask if our appearance is a good witness of Christianity. Does it identify us with rebellion? Could it be a stumbling block to others? Or is it an example of godliness both to unbelievers and believers?

Colored makeup and tattoos are contrary to the principle of avoiding personal ornamentation and vanity. Christian woman are encouraged to adorn themselves—that is, to present themselves as neat, clean, and attractive—but they must do so with "shamefacedness and sobriety" (I Timothy 2:9). "Shamefacedness" means respect, reverence, self-restraint, modesty, or bashfulness toward men; not being bold or forward.

Makeup is obviously designed to attract the opposite sex. It does so by accentuating sensuality in the woman and arousing lust in the man. The application of makeup is not arbitrary, but much of it originated as an imitation of a woman's appearance during sexual arousal. Thus, both in the Old Testament and throughout history, painting the face is associated with brazenness, forwardness, seduction, and prostitution.

According to history, painting of the eyelids to enhance sexual appeal was first introduced in ancient Egypt about 3000 BC. Proverbs 6:25 refers to this practice: "Lust not after her beauty in thine heart; neither let her take thee with her eyelids." The surrounding verses speak of this woman as "evil," "strange," "whorish," and an "adulteress."

A prominent example occurs in II Kings 9:30. Jehu was anointed king of Israel and given the mission of destroying the family of Ahab, who hated God's Word. Jezebel, the wife of Ahab, heard that Jehu was coming and tried to seduce him in order to save her own life. As a means of enticing him, she painted her face or eyes and adorned her head. When Jehu arrived, he discerned her strategy and ordered her to be killed.

Esther, the woman who saved her nation, stands in sharp contrast to Jezebel. The young women who appeared before the Persian king made preparations with oils and perfumes. When they went before the king, they could ask for anything else that they wanted to assist them, and no doubt they chose various cosmetics and ornaments. When Esther's turn came, she asked for nothing but relied on the advice of the king's chamberlain who had charge of the women. (See Esther 2:13-15.) She wanted to be accepted for who she was, and she relied on the will of the Lord.

In Jeremiah 4:30, God compared the backslidden nation of Judah to a woman who tried to appeal to her lovers with makeup and ornaments. Ezekiel 23:36-44 similarly describes Samaria and Jerusalem (the capitals of Israel and Judah) as two women who adorned themselves with makeup and jewelry in order to commit adultery with a variety of lovers. In both cases, God associated makeup with sexual immorality. Nowhere does the Bible associate makeup with a virtuous woman. Of course, most women today who wear makeup do not have the intention of being immoral but are simply conforming to culture. Nevertheless, these passages of Scripture reveal what God thinks about ornamental makeup. When we abstain from makeup and tattoos, we please Him.

In American society before the twentieth century, women generally did not wear makeup, and those who did were considered to be immoral. According to *Ency-*

clopedia Britannica, it was not until after World War I that makeup became generally acceptable, and even then its use was limited until after World War II. Most conservative churches did not approve of it until that time.

Ornamental jewelry. Wearing of ornamental jewelry violates the principle of avoiding personal ornamentation and the principle of moderation in cost. Under the inspiration of the Holy Spirit, both the apostle Paul and the apostle Peter addressed this aspect of adornment. "To adorn" means to decorate, ornament, beautify, or embellish. According to I Timothy 2:9-10, women are to adorn themselves in modest clothing and with good works, but not with "broided hair, or gold, or pearls, or costly array." Similarly, I Peter 3:3-4 says their adorning should be with "the hidden man of the heart, in that which is not corruptible, even the ornament of a meek and quiet spirit, which is in the sight of God of great price"; it should not be "that outward adorning of plaiting the hair, and of wearing of gold, or of putting on of apparel."

These two passages support each other. Both warn against braided or plaited hair, which refers to the elaborate hair arrangement of that time, particularly to the intertwining of pearls and gold thread in the hair. Both warn against ornamental jewelry, both using the example of a precious metal and one using the example of a precious stone. Both warn against extravagant clothing; the "outward adorning . . . of putting on of apparel" in I Peter refers to clothing worn as excessive ornamentation instead of for practical reasons of modesty and protection from the elements.

While the foregoing New Testament passages provide the most complete and relevant teaching on adornment for Christians today, God sought to introduce similar principles in the Old Testament.

In Exodus 33:1-11, the Israelites had just sinned by making a golden calf and worshiping it. God had promised to lead them personally into the land of Canaan, but His justice now compelled Him not to appear in their midst lest He consume them. In His mercy, God promised to send an angel to lead them instead. When the people heard this, they began to mourn. As a sign of their sorrow and their repentance, they did not put on their ornaments. The Lord told them they were a stubborn people and instructed, "Put off thy ornaments from thee." In response, they "stripped themselves of their ornaments." They needed to strip themselves of their vanity in the presence of God.

Moses then walked toward the Tabernacle, and all the people stood in the doors of their tents to watch. As a result of their consecration, the Lord came down in a cloud of glory. All the people worshiped Him, and He talked to Moses as a friend. The stripping of unnecessary ornaments had demonstrated that the Israelites really wanted the presence of God. It was a lesson in self-denial and humility. Likewise, if we want the fullness of God's presence and a close relationship with Him as a body of believers, we need to make this type of consecration.

Isaiah 3:16-26 describes the vanity of wearing ornaments. The nation of Judah had become proud, which displeased God. Consequently, He said He would remove all their ornaments. The passage lists the ornaments and expensive apparel that displayed their pride. (Definitions are from Strong's *Concordance* or from the New King James Version where indicated.) They were tinkling ornaments for the feet, cauls (netting for the hair), round tires like the moon (round pendants for the neck, or "crescents" in NKJV), chains (pendants for the ear), bracelets, mufflers (long veils), bonnets (headdresses), ornaments for the legs, headbands, tablets ("perfume boxes" in NKJV), earrings (or "charms" in NKJV), rings, nose jewels, changeable suits of apparel ("festal apparel" in NKJV), mantles (cloaks), wimples (wide cloths), crisping pins ("purses" in NKJV), glasses (mirrors), fine linen, hoods (headdresses), veils, and stomachers (figured mantles for holidays). The various garments and the purses were costly and usually were embroidered elaborately. The mirrors and perfume boxes were often hung from the neck or girdle and worn as ornaments. All of these things have the potential for vanity, and in this case the primary reason for wearing them was pride.

From the foregoing passages in the Old and New Testaments, we learn that our appearance and dress should display humility, modesty, and moderation. We should not wear ornamental jewelry or costly, extravagant clothing. In making decisions about what is appropriate, we should ask, Is this item flashy or gaudy? What is my motive for wearing it? Does it serve a useful purpose? Even if it serves a useful purpose, is it extravagant? Should I consider a less extravagant or less showy alternative? Is God asking me to make a consecration in this area so that I can draw closer to Him?

For example, earrings, necklaces, and bracelets are exclusively ornamental, while a watch is primarily functional rather than ornamental. Even a watch could become ostentatious and vain, however.

If possible, Christians should dress well and in good

taste. It is often advisable to spend a greater amount of money for clothing of higher quality, yet we can do so without dressing ostentatiously. Most often, those who are simply and tastefully dressed are the most elegant.

Leaders should carefully consider these teachings and develop personal convictions based on Scripture. They should recognize that their choices in this area will influence others. Indeed, the rest of the congregation will tend to take more liberties than the leaders. Thus, if leaders wear a small item of jewelry that they think is acceptable, followers will tend to wear larger items that are questionable or unacceptable. It is advisable, therefore, for leaders to be somewhat stricter on themselves than what they might expect the congregation to be. When in doubt, all Christians, and especially leaders, should choose alternatives that lead to greater consecration and holiness rather than to the possibility of greater worldliness.

Guidelines for children. The Bible says, "Train up a child in the way he should go: and when he is old, he will not depart from it" (Proverbs 22:6). We should teach holiness to our children. In choosing and allowing their dress, we should implement the principles of modesty, not using personal ornaments, moderation in cost, distinction between male and female, and separation from the world. Before puberty, modesty is not as significant an issue. Some types of clothing that would be immodest on adults are not immodest on children. Nevertheless, we should not dress children in seductive or provocative styles, as this would be inappropriate and would establish a detrimental precedent for when they grow older.

A witness in early church history. It is interesting to note that despite differences of doctrine and the influx of false doctrines, Christians of the second and third centuries generally continued to adhere to scriptural teachings on adornment and dress. For example, in the third century AD, Tertullian wrote a treatise entitled *On Female Dress*.[3] In it, he taught against rouge, hair dye, wigs, elaborate hair styling for men and women, eyeliner, jewels, and ornaments. He called Christians to temperance and sacrifice. He said that if God treats lust like fornication, then He will not fail to punish those who deliberately arouse lust in others by their dress. He also noted that the person who is accustomed to luxury, jewels, and ornaments will not be willing to sacrifice all, including life itself, for the cause of Christ. Tertullian wrote:

> You must not overstep the line to which simple and sufficient elegance limits its desires, the line which is pleasing to God. Against Him those women sin who torment their skin with potions, stain their cheeks with rouge, and extend the line of their eyes with black coloring. Doubtless they are dissatisfied with God's plastic skill. . . . Take not to yourself such robes and garments as play the part of pimp and pander. . . . Let us cast away earthly ornaments, if we desire heavenly.

Throughout church history, many revivalists and reformers advocated similar teachings concerning adornment and dress, including the Anabaptists, John Calvin (Reformed leader), John Wesley (Methodist leader), the Holiness movement, and the Pentecostal movement. For further discussion, see *Practical Holiness: A Second Look* by David K. Bernard.

A contemporary non-Pentecostal witness. It is also interesting to discover that in our day conservative Christians from various backgrounds have embraced these truths of God's Word and made similar applications. The following information is taken from an Italo-American evangelical theologian, Dr. Samuele Bacchiocchi. While we would not agree with all his beliefs and positions, he bears witness to important principles of Scripture in this area.[4]

- "Dress and appearance are an important index of Christian character."
- "Adorning our bodies with colorful cosmetics, glittering jewelry, and luxurious clothes reveals inner pride and vanity, which are destructive to ourselves and to others."
- "To experience inner spiritual renewal and reconciliation with God, it is necessary to remove all outward besetting objects of idolatry, including jewelry and ornaments."
- "Christians should dress in a modest and decent way, showing respect for God, themselves, and others. . . . The purpose of modesty is not only to prevent lustful desires, but also to preserve something which is very fragile and yet fundamental to the survival of a marital relationship: the ability to maintain a deep, intimate relationship with one's spouse."
- "Christians should dress soberly, restraining any desire to exhibit themselves by wearing eye-catching clothes, cosmetics, or jewelry."
- "Wearing finger rings is not compatible with the Biblical principles of modesty; historically, they

have tempted people to wear all kinds of jewelry. . . . The wearing of the signet ring is not condemned in the Bible, presumably because it was regarded as an instrument of authority rather than an ornament. . . . People can become so enamored with their finger ring that they are easily tempted to wear all kinds of jewelry. To play it safe, it is advisable not to wear a wedding ring, unless it is a social imperative."

- "Christians should respect gender distinctions in clothing by wearing clothes that affirm their male or female identities." "Pants still have a masculine connotation and do not affirm the gender distinctions [for women]." He offered some exceptions, however, in situations involving cold weather, housework, recreation, or sports, as long as the choice of clothing will still "affirm gender distinctions and look decent."

The challenge today. The final decision rests with us. Will we retain biblical teachings on modesty, humility, and moderation in outward appearance? Will we maintain distinction of the sexes and separation from the world? Or will we succumb to the pressures of the world and its so-called modernization, which is really a revival of ancient evils? Will we identify with God or with the world? May God help us to uphold the complete message of holiness. May God help us to keep the landmarks established by the Word of God, the teaching of our spiritual forefathers, and the leading of the Spirit.

Notes

[1]W. E. Vine, *An Expository Dictionary of New Testament*

Words (Old Tappan, NJ: Revell, 1940).

[2]Claudia Brush Kidwell and Valerie Steele, *Men and Women: Dressing the Part* (Washington: Smithsonian Institution Press, 1989), pl. 2, pp. 7, 144-46.

[3]Anne Fremantle, ed. *A Treasury of Early Christianity* (New York: Viking Press, 1953).

[4]Samuele Bacchiocchi, *Christian Dress and Adornment* (Berrien Springs, MI: Biblical Perspectives, 1995), 155, 160-169. For partial text, see online: http://www.biblicalperspectives.com.

CHAPTER

7

Bible Truths Concerning Hair

If a man have long hair, it is a shame unto him[.] But if a woman have long hair, it is a glory to her: for her hair is given her for a covering (I Corinthians 11:14-15).

We find the New Testament teaching about hair in I Corinthians 11:1-16. This passage plainly teaches that a woman should have long, uncut hair and a man should have short hair. At the outset, let us briefly summarize the reasons for this teaching.

Reasons why a woman should have long hair

1. Long hair is a sign of her submission to authority.
2. The angels are watching to see if she has this sign.
3. It is a shame for a woman to pray or prophesy with an uncovered head, for she thereby dishonors her

head (authority). Long hair is her symbolic head covering. If she shears (cuts) her hair it is like shaving her head.

4. Nature teaches her to have long hair as opposed to shorn (cut) hair or a shaved head.
5. Long hair is a woman's glory.
6. It is one of God's methods for maintaining a distinction between male and female.

Reasons why a man should have short hair

1. Short hair on a man is a symbol of his position of authority and his submission to Christ's authority.
2. A man who prays or prophesies with his head covered by long hair dishonors his head (authority), which is Christ.
3. Nature teaches him to have short hair.
4. Long hair is a shame on a man.
5. It is one of God's methods for maintaining a distinction between male and female.

To fully understand and appreciate these reasons, we need to look at the significance of hair in the Old Testament. The Old Testament was written for our learning, example, and admonition (Romans 15:4; I Corinthians 10:11). The law served as a schoolmaster to bring people to Christ (Galatians 3:24). The Old Testament contains many types and shadows that help us to appreciate and understand the meaning of the New Testament (Colossians 2:16-17; Hebrews 8:5; 10:1).

Hair was a symbol of perfection and strength. Among the Jews, an abundance of hair indicated perfection and strength. Lack of hair symbolized the opposite: imperfection, lost glory, and powerlessness. For example, the young men in II Kings 2:23 contemptuously called Elisha a bald head. This expression did not necessarily indicate actual baldness but meant that the person so called was worthless, imperfect, and without glory.

Cutting of hair was a symbol of disgrace or mourning. Throughout the Old Testament, the cutting of hair symbolized disgrace (Ezra 9:3; Nehemiah 13:25) or mourning (Isaiah 22:12; Ezekiel 27:31; 29:18; Micah 1:16). The loss of hair signified barrenness, sin and the judgment of God (Isaiah 3:17, 24; 15:2; Jeremiah 47:5; 48:37; Ezekiel 7:18; Amos 8:10). In Isaiah 3:17-24, the judgment pronounced on proud women was that instead of having well-set hair they would be struck bald by God. In essence, they would be without honor and would be ashamed. In Jeremiah 7:29, God used cut hair as a symbol of Judah's backslidden condition and her rejection by God.

Hair was a symbol of glory. A woman's long hair symbolizes the blessings of God in Ezekiel 16:7. Gray hair is a crown of glory (Proverbs 16:31). God told Ezekiel to cut his hair as an object lesson of God's judgment on Judah (Ezekiel 5:1-4, 12). He then showed Ezekiel that His glory would depart from the Temple in Jerusalem (Ezekiel 10:3-10). Ezekiel without hair signified Ezekiel without glory, which in turn symbolized Jerusalem without the glory of God.

Uncut hair was a mark of separation unto God. When we study the vow of the Nazarites (or, more accurately, Nazirites), we discover that hair could be a mark of separation (Numbers 6:1-21). This name comes from the Hebrew *nazir*, which means "separate, i.e. consecrated."[1] The Nazarites were separated unto Jehovah as shown by three outward signs. A Nazarite was not to partake of grapes or any product of grapes, was not to touch a corpse, and was not to cut the hair on the head. This last sign was the only one that immediately identified a Nazarite by outward appearance.

Either a man or a woman could be a Nazarite (verse 2). The Nazarite vow could be taken for a temporary period or for a lifetime. Paul took temporary vows, while Samson was a Nazarite from his mother's womb (Acts 21:20-27; Judges 13:7). Since abundance of hair signified strength, perfection, and glory, the free growth of hair on the head represented the dedication of all one's strength and power to God. The hair was "the consecration of his God upon his head" (Numbers 6:7).

The Nazarites could not cut their hair at all, but they let it grow. During their period of separation they were holy. At the end of the vow they cut their hair (verse 5). The reason they could not defile themselves by touching a corpse was that the mark of their separation was on their head for all to see (verse 7). If Nazarites broke their vow by becoming defiled, they had to shave their head (verse 9). The reason is that their long hair would signify that they were still separated, while their actions proved otherwise. Their appearance and actions would be in conflict.

If Nazarites broke their vow, they had to begin all over again (verse 12). Their prior commitment was not counted if the vow was broken. (See also Ezekiel 3:20; 18:24; 33:12-13.) When the vow was completed, their hair was cut and put on the altar for a peace offering (verse 18). It was called the hair of separation unto God (verse 19).

Each seventh year in Israel was called a sabbatical year. Trees and vines were not pruned, and fields were not plowed or sown. In particular, grape vines were left undressed (Leviticus 25:5, 11). In Hebrew, the word "undressed" is *nazir*, the same word translated as "Nazarite" in Numbers. In fact, a second definition of this word is "an unpruned vine (like an unshorn Nazarite)."[2] These "Nazarite" vines were not cut or pruned but were allowed to grow freely, just like the Nazarites' hair.

In summary, in the Old Testament hair was often a symbol of power, perfection, and glory. The absence of hair could signify worthlessness and glory departed. Christians today are not Nazarites in the literal sense, but our study has shown that the hair of the Nazarites was a visible mark of separation from the world and consecration to God.

New Testament teaching. We now turn to the New Testament teaching on hair as found in I Corinthians 11:1-16. Most denominational churches ignore this passage, concluding that it does not apply today. Some interpret it to mean that women must pray with some type of cloth on their heads. Most conservative churches at one time taught women to have long hair, and some continue to do so today.

All Scripture is given by the inspiration of God (II Timothy 3:16). We should not ignore any passage of Scripture, for each is precious and important. We should especially heed instructions to the New Testament church, for we are part of that church. Let us analyze this passage of Scripture in that light.

Verses 1-2. Paul admonished believers to follow him and to keep the ordinances or teachings that he had delivered to them. Among these ordinances is his teaching concerning hair in the subsequent verses.

Verse 3. God is the head of Christ. As a human, Jesus submitted to the eternal Spirit of God that dwelt in Him, thereby setting an example for us. Christ subjected His flesh to the plan and purpose of God, even unto death (Philippians 2:8).

Similarly, Christ is the head of the man, and the man is the head of the woman. God intends for the man to be the leader of the family. He is to be the spiritual representative of the home. In the beginning, God held Adam primarily accountable for human sinfulness. The sins of fathers particularly affect children (Exodus 20:5). Moreover, a woman is to respect the leadership of her own husband (Ephesians 5:22; Colossians 3:18; I Peter 3:1).

Verse 4. A man should not have his head covered when he prays or prophesies. If he does, he dishonors his head or leader, namely, Christ. Prophesying includes any anointed preaching and testimony.

Verse 5. A woman who prays or prophesies (including preaching and testimony) with her head uncovered dishonors her head or leader, which is the man. In other words, the sexes should not try to change places. The woman's covering is a sign of her role in God's plan. According to verse 15, long hair is the symbolic covering that God has given her, and according to verse 6 it should be unshorn or uncut.

Verse 6. If a woman is not going to cover her head (by letting her hair grow long), then this is equivalent to cutting off her hair. But this is a disgrace or a shame to her. It signifies the taking away of her glory in God's sight. Since it is a shame for her hair to be shorn (cut) or shaved, she should be covered (let her hair grow long).

Verses 7-9. Adam was created in the image of God and subsequently Eve was also (Genesis 1:26-27). The man is the representative of the family before God, with the authority and responsibility to provide for his family, protect his family, and lead his family spiritually. As a sign of his position, his head should not be covered (with long hair, verse 14). The woman originally came from the man (Genesis 2:22). She is his partner, a helper comparable to him (Genesis 2:20), who respects his position and follows his godly leadership. Woman is the crowning glory of man. To demonstrate this relationship, her head should be covered (verse 6) with her glory, which is her long hair (verse 15). In short, male and female are equally important in God's plan, but their roles are distinct, and God wants this distinction to be displayed and preserved outwardly by their hair.

Verse 10. The angels are involved with this subject, as they observe the obedience or disobedience of humans to God's plan. The angels desire to look into our salvation (I Peter 1:12). Pride and rebellion caused the fall of Satan and many angels (I Timothy 3:6; Isaiah 14:12-15). Thus, a woman should have "power" on her head as an example to the angels. The Greek word here is *exousia*, meaning "authority," and in this context it indicates a mark or sign of authority. The angels look to see if women have the sign of consecration, submission, and power with God, or if they are rebellious like Satan. Women's hair shows the angels whether or not the church is submissive to Christ, the head of the church.

Verses 11-12. Women are not inferior to men, and men are not complete without women. Both depend on each other. This principle of complementarity and interdependence is especially true in the church. The roles are different, however, and God has designated the man to be the leader of the family.

Verse 13. Paul used a question as a part of his teaching method. Is it proper for a woman to pray to God uncovered? His answer is no; it is a shame for her to do so (verse 5).

Verse 14. Nature, not just custom, teaches a man to have short hair but a woman to have long hair. Since God is the Creator of nature, the teaching of nature in this situation comes from God. God's purpose is to make a distinction of the sexes in this area.

Verse 15. A woman's hair is given for her glory and for a covering to satisfy the requirements of the preceding verses. This verse does not mention any other covering such as a hat or scarf. It would be difficult for a woman to put on a scarf every time she prays or witnesses to someone, especially if she prays without ceasing (I Thessalonians 5:17). This verse explains that a woman does not have to wear a veil of cloth; her hair is sufficient covering.

The Greek word for "have long hair" here is *komaō*, which means "wear long hair, let one's hair grow long"[3] or "wear tresses of hair."[4] The word for "covered" in verse 6 is *katakaluptō*, meaning "to cover wholly, i.e., to veil."[5] The word for "covering" in verse 15 is *peribolaion*, which is "something thrown around one, i.e., a mantle, veil."[6] Thus, verses 5-6 teach that a woman's head should be covered wholly or veiled. Verse 15 says her hair is a mantle or veil; it is a symbolic article of apparel for the head. Clearly, long hair is the covering that meets the requirements of verses 5, 6, and 13.

Verse 16. The people of God are not contentious. The church has no custom of being contentious over the teachings of God's Word. It has no custom regarding hair other than what Paul had just described. Some say this verse means that if anyone disagrees with these teachings then obedience is not required. If this were true, however, then Paul's entire teaching in this section would be in vain, and he would be condoning contention and disobedience. Paul would not say, "If you do not have such a custom, then you are not required to obey the Word of God and the ordinances of the church." Reading verses 2 and 16 together, the message is that we should obey these teachings instead of being contentious.

Reasons for biblical teaching on hair. Hair symbolizes the relationship of husband and wife, which in turn represents the Lord's relationship with the church. A woman's long hair symbolizes that she submits to God's plan and to the family leadership of her husband. It is her glory. It is a sign to the angels of her commitment to God and her power with God. It is a covering so that she can pray and prophesy publicly without being ashamed. Similarly, a man's short hair symbolizes that he submits to God's plan and accepts the family leadership position.

Nature teaches women to let their hair grow long and men to cut their hair short. First, nature teaches that there should be a visible distinction between male and female. Second, in almost all cultures, men have worn short hair in comparison to women. Third, men are ten times more likely to go bald than women. It is natural for a man not to have any hair but unnatural for a woman not to have hair. Therefore, when men and women follow the biblical teaching on hair, they follow God's plan as established in creation. Hair length makes a distinction between the sexes, which God considers to be important. (See Deuteronomy 22:5.) It is also a mark of separation from the world. (See chapter 6.)

God always gives us a choice to do His will or not. He never forces us to be what He wants us to be. We did not choose to be male or female, however; that choice was determined for us at conception. By our choice of dress and hairstyle, we show acceptance or rejection of God's plan for us as male or female, husband or wife, father or mother. The roles are equally important in family, church, and society, but they are different. God wants us to demonstrate our willingness to accept the roles He has chosen for us.

The relationship between husband and wife is like that between Christ and the church. The husband is the head of the wife as Christ is head of the church (Ephesians 5:22-23). Therefore, when Christian men and women demonstrate their acceptance of God's plan by their hair, they also demonstrate the church's submission to Christ.

How long is long? Our study of the Nazarites indicates that long hair as a mark of separation means uncut hair or hair that is allowed to grow freely. By letting the hair grow freely, women allow nature, the teacher that Paul appealed to in I Corinthians 11:14, to determine the proper length for each individual. The Greek word for long hair in verse 15 means that a woman should let her hair grow long. Moreover, verse 6 indicates that if a woman cuts her hair, it is the same as if she shaves her head. The Bible does not provide any other definition for long hair on women, nor does it designate any particular measurement as long. The point is not to grow it to a certain length, because different individuals' hair naturally grows to different lengths. If a woman does not cut her hair, then it is long in God's sight. Finally, the fundamental principle is that a woman's hair needs to be visibly longer than that of men.

A man's hair should be at least short enough to distinguish him from women. This length may vary somewhat in various ages and cultures. In determining the appropriate length of a man's hair we should consider the following questions. Is it shorter than that of the average woman in our society? Is it a good witness, or is it a reproach to the church and to Christ? Is it a sign of rebellion against authority in the community or in the church? Is it a stumbling block or an offense to other members of the church? (See I Corinthians 8:9-13.) Does it identify him with elements of the world from which he has been saved?

Under certain cultural circumstances, all but the first of these questions could apply to facial hair also. Whether shaved or allowed to grow, a man's beard is a sign of masculinity. In general, facial hair was highly regarded in the Bible and in many other times and cultures, but in white, middle-class America of the 1960s it became a sign of rebellion. In the Bible, we find positive examples both of shaving and growing beards. (See Genesis 41:14; Psalm 133:2.)

The notion that Jesus had long, womanly hair is a myth. He was not a Nazarite as some believe, but a Nazarene, which means an inhabitant of the city of Nazareth. He drank the fruit of the vine and touched corpses, so He did not have a Nazarite vow. The art that shows Him with long hair was painted many centuries later and is without scriptural or historical foundation. It reflects medieval rather than biblical customs. Roman sculpture and coinage as well as other historical sources show that men generally wore short hair in Christ's day. In any case, He would not have worn womanly hair in contradiction to the Word of God.

Dyeing the hair. According to Proverbs 16:31, gray hair is a crown of glory. Jesus Himself assumed that people would not change the color of their hair (Matthew 5:36). The same reasons for not wearing makeup as discussed in chapter 6 also teach us not to dye our hair. What is the difference between painting the cheeks, eyebrows, or eyelashes and dyeing the hair? Similarly, these principles indicate that we should not use false eyelashes or wigs that seek to change the natural appearance. The proper course for both men and women is not to change the natural color of one's hair.

Attitudes. There are two concerns regarding a woman's attitude toward long hair. Some may resent the need to care for and fix long hair. But with moderate effort it is possible to fix long hair so that it looks modern, neat, and attractive. Many promise to do anything for the Lord, yet when it comes to long hair, they are unwilling to make the effort. Since God has made His wishes clear, disobeying Him demonstrates self-centeredness, a lack of consecration, and a lack of love.

Another danger is pride. It is possible to take the very hair that is supposed to be a sign of submission and arrange it in an ostentatious display. Overly elaborate hairdos and extravagant hairpieces draw attention to self rather than the message of the long hair. Such ostentation undermines the purpose and testimony of the long hair. Many people have been impressed with the beautiful, holy, long hair of Christian women, but others have been perplexed, confused, and repelled by showy displays.

Thus I Timothy 2:9 warns women not to adorn themselves with "broided hair," which, according to the Amplified Bible, includes "[elaborate] hair arrangement." We find the same admonition in I Peter 3:3. Both verses refer to elaborate hair arrangement in the first century, such as braiding the hair with a string of pearls or with gold coins attached to silk cords. We must exercise moderation and temperance in all things, including hair arrangement. It would be a shame for a woman to undermine the message of holiness with something intended to be a sign of holiness.

Shall we obey I Corinthians 11:1-16? We cannot treat this passage casually, merely because we think it is outdated or inconvenient. If we ignore it, then what is to prevent us from ignoring the teaching about communion in the same chapter or any other passage of Scripture?

Some may consider disobedience in this matter to be a minor thing. No doubt Moses thought it was a minor thing to disobey God by striking a rock to obtain water instead of speaking to the rock. After all, he had stricken a rock to obtain water once before at God's command. Yet God did not allow him to enter the Promised Land because he did not obey His instruction to speak to the rock on the second occasion. (See Exodus 17:6; Numbers 20:7-12.) In God's plan, the rock represented Christ (I Corinthians 10:4), who was smitten once for us and whose grace is now available whenever we simply speak

His name in faith. Although Moses had no way of understanding this significance, he should have simply obeyed God's plan, and he paid a severe price for not doing so. It is always important to obey God's Word in all things.

Ministers cannot be neutral concerning God's Word. Pastors must teach God's commands to their people, or both pastors and people will be accountable to God. Pastors must study the Scriptures and ask God for wisdom and knowledge. Once they understand God's Word, they must preach and teach it. Otherwise, they are hirelings—ministers who preach for money or for the applause of the people. True shepherds will love their people enough to preach truth even though some may not want to hear it. They will love all the Word of God, not just a part of it. They will not condone disobedience by appointing leaders who deliberately ignore or rebel against part of the Word. Those who decide not teach part of the Word should not teach at all, or they will have a greater condemnation (James 3:1).

Regardless of personal inconvenience or the opinions of others, it is our responsibility and privilege to serve God. Doing so is the very definition of true love. Jesus said, "If you love me, keep my commandments" (John 14:15).

Notes

[1]James Strong, *Exhaustive Concordance of the Bible* (Nashville: Abingdon, 1890).

[2]Ibid.

[3]Walter Bauer et al., *A Greek-English Lexicon of the New Testament*, 2nd ed. (Chicago: University of Chicago Press, 1979).

[4]Strong.

[5]Ibid.

[6]Ibid.

CHAPTER

8

The Temple of God

What? know ye not that your body is the temple of the Holy Ghost which is in you? . . . If any man defile the temple of God, him shall God destroy (I Corinthians 6:19; 3:17).

The body. The body is a temple, or dwelling place, for the Spirit of God. For this reason, we are not to defile the body but are to keep it holy. In the broadest application, we are not to commit sin with our physical bodies, and we are to protect the collective body of Christ, which is the church. In this chapter, we will restrict our discussion to specific activities that harm and defile our physical bodies. We will particularly discuss the application of these principles to food, alcoholic beverages, tobacco, and drugs.

Food. Immediately after the Creation, God gave to humans all vegetables, grains, and fruits for food, with the exception of the tree of knowledge of good and evil (Genesis 1:29; 2:16-17). After the Flood, God explained that humans could eat every living thing, both plants and animals, with the exception of blood (Genesis 9:1-4). In both instances, God retained one thing as a symbol of His lordship. While He specified that humans could eat meat, He prohibited them from eating blood because it is a symbol of life and He alone is the giver of life.

The law of Moses restricted the diet of Israel in several ways. (See Leviticus 11; Deuteronomy 14.) God allowed the Israelites to eat all animals that both chewed the cud and had a divided hoof (Leviticus 11:3). Animals forbidden by this rule were the camel, coney, hare, and pig. Aquatic animals without scales and fins were also unclean (Leviticus 11:10). Twenty kinds of birds, mostly scavengers and birds of prey, were unclean (Leviticus 11:13-19). All flying, creeping things—i.e., insects—were unclean with the exception of the locust, the bald locust, the beetle (or cricket, NKJV and NIV), and the grasshopper.

The main purpose of these dietary laws was to separate Israel from all other nations. They also helped to protect the Israelites from unsanitary and disease-carrying food. In those days, medical information about germs was unknown while sanitation was primitive by modern standards, so these laws promoted health. For example, pork is a well-known source of trichinosis if it is not cooked properly.

In Acts 15 the leaders of the New Testament church met to establish which restrictions of the Jewish law apply to Gentiles. The moral teachings were not an issue, because everyone knew that they were the same in every age, but they discussed ceremonial laws such as circumcision. They decided that Gentile Christians did not need to be circumcised but needed to keep four points of the Jewish law:

1. *Abstain from food offered to idols*. We are not to have anything to do with idol worship. We are not to participate in idolatrous festivals or eat food in situations that would give seeming endorsement of idolatry.

2. *Abstain from fornication*. This word covers all types of sexual intercourse outside marriage, including premarital sex, adultery, and homosexuality. (See chapter 9.) This statement is probably included here to make sure that the Gentiles would define fornication according to the provisions of the law of Moses instead of by pagan beliefs. For instance, the Gentiles needed to know the definition of incest according to the law of Moses (Leviticus 18:6-18).

3. *Abstain from things strangled*. The reference is to Leviticus 17:13-14. When an animal is killed, it must be butchered so that the blood drains out of the carcass. If an animal is merely strangled, the blood remains in it, and anyone who eats the meat would be eating blood, which is forbidden.

4. *Abstain from blood*. As discussed below, we are not to eat blood, because it represents life. This command teaches us that life is sacred, and therefore we should abstain from bloodshed—the taking of human life. (See chapter 10.)

Acts 15 does not mention any of the Jewish laws concerning unclean animals. Consequently, Christians are free to eat anything except for blood and, in certain situations, food offered to idols. The Old Testament laws concerning food were a shadow of things to come. They signify Christians' need to distinguish between clean and unclean things in a moral sense and to separate themselves from everything that is spiritually unclean. But Christians are not bound by the specific dietary laws of Moses. "Let no man therefore judge you in meat, or in drink, . . . which are a shadow of things to come; but the body is of Christ" (Colossians 2:16-17).

In the last days some teachers will start "forbidding to marry, and commanding to abstain from meats, which God hath created to be received with thanksgiving of them which believe and know the truth" (I Timothy 4:3). Such teaching against marriage and against certain types of food is contrary to the will of God. Marriage is sanctified by the Word of God, and all foods are sanctified by thanksgiving and prayer (verses 4-5). There is no New Testament restriction on certain kinds of food.

Blood. Eating blood or eating the meat of a strangled animal, which retains a significant amount of blood, is still prohibited for Christians. This restriction began before the law of Moses and continues after it. (See Genesis 9:4; Leviticus 7:26; 17:10-14; Deuteronomy 12:23-25; Acts 15:20, 29; 21:25.) The reason is that the life of an animal or a human is in the blood (Leviticus 17:14). Modern science has verified this statement by the discovery that blood carries life-giving oxygen and nutrition to all parts of the body. In every age, God has chosen blood to represent life and to represent the remission of sins (Hebrews 9:22). Consequently, we are not to eat blood.

Food offered to idols. We find additional teaching on this subject in I Corinthians 8:1-13 and 10:23-33. As Christians, we know that an idol is nothing and that there is only one God. Therefore, eating food offered to an idol will not harm us. Nevertheless, we must exercise our liberty in this area with caution, so that others do not misinterpret our actions. We must not give anyone the impression that we participate in or condone idol worship.

Therefore, we must not eat at a feast where the food has been offered to idols, and we must not prepare food to offer to idols. If idolaters see us knowingly participate in such activities, they will think we are worshiping idols. Moreover, if fellow believers who are weak (that is, who do not have full Christian knowledge of this subject) see us eating this food, our actions may become a stumbling block to them. In both cases, we harm other people by our liberty.

Let us suppose, however, that someone gives us food which, unknown to us, has been offered to an idol. If we eat it, have we sinned? No, because idols are nothing. In the first century, so much food was offered to idols in pagan temples that the priests could not eat it all. They sold the excess food in the markets. The question arose among Christians as to whether it would be a sin to eat this food. If so, how could they tell if the food sold in the markets had been offered to idols or not?

Paul answered, "Whatsoever is sold in the shambles [markets] that eat, asking no question for conscience sake" (I Corinthians 10:25). Similarly, what if Christians are invited to a home or a feast where food may have previously been offered to idols. Paul answered, "Whatsoever is set before you, eat, asking no question for conscience sake" (verse 27). If the food is offered to idols at the feast, however, or the Christians are told that the food has been dedicated to idols, then they should not partake.

They should abstain for the sake of those who are watching them (verses 28-29). We should keep in mind that demons accept the worship that is offered to idols, so for that reason we cannot become associated with idolatry in any way (verse 20).

Temperance and gluttony. Christians are to be temperate and moderate in their eating habits. We should practice good eating habits to preserve our health and strength, and we should refrain from foods that affect us adversely.

We should not be guilty of gluttony—eating to excess. Excessive eating can be sinful (Deuteronomy 21:20; Proverbs 23:21). Proverbs 25:16 teaches us to be temperate and moderate in eating. Jesus warned us not to be "overcharged with surfeiting," which includes eating excessively or to the point of nausea (Luke 21:34). Some people refuse to drink alcohol or smoke cigarettes because these substances are harmful to the body, but they literally eat themselves to death. Overeating and improper eating can cause a variety of diseases and eventually a premature death.

This is an abuse of the temple of God. What impression do we make on sinners if we condemn intemperance and overindulgence in some areas while being equally guilty in the area of eating? What kind of image do ministers present if they are grossly overweight from too much eating and too little exercise? We have Christian liberty in the area of food, but we must also follow our common sense and the leading of the Spirit.

We are to be "temperate in all things" (I Corinthians 9:25). Temperance means moderation and self-control. It should be our watchword when we consider any physical activity or fleshly emotion. Those who rule their spirit are better than those who conquer a city (Proverbs 16:32). Those who do not rule their spirit are like a city without defenses (Proverbs 25:28). We must keep our bodies under subjection (I Corinthians 9:27). We must not yield our bodies to anything but the Spirit of God (Romans 6:12-13).

For these reasons, we abstain from anything that would cause us to lose control of ourselves or remove us from the guidance of the Holy Spirit, either permanently by addiction or temporarily by intoxication. Paul explained the proper exercise of Christian liberty in this matter: "All things are lawful unto me, but all things are not expedient [beneficial, helpful]: all things are lawful for me, but I will not be brought under the power of any" (I Corinthians 6:12). If we yield to ourselves to something, then we become its servant (Romans 6:16). If we allow ourselves to become addicted or intoxicated, then we undermine our defense against sin, and God cannot use us as He wills.

Beverages. The law was lenient concerning drinks (Deuteronomy 14:26), yet the Old Testament warns against intoxicating drinks (Proverbs 20:1; Isaiah 5:11). The New Testament says that whatever we eat or drink, we should do it for the glory of God (I Corinthians 10:31). In considering what to eat or drink, we should ask, "Can I eat or drink this to the glory of God?"

Coffee, tea, and most carbonated beverages are mild stimulants because they contain caffeine. Medical research reveals that under normal circumstances caffeine is not harmful. However, if we become nervous, irritable, weak, sick, or unable to fast unless we get our morning cup of coffee or our daily soft drink, then we should carefully evaluate our use. We do not need any habit that controls or dictates to us. If any substance causes harmful side effects or is habit forming, we must learn to control it.

Alcoholic beverages. "Wine is a mocker, strong drink is raging: and whosoever is deceived thereby is not wise" (Proverbs 20:1). "Look not thou upon the wine when it is red, when it giveth his colour in the cup, when it moveth itself aright" (Proverbs 23:31). This statement is a clear warning against drinking wine after it has fermented and has become intoxicating. The evil consequences of drinking wine and mixed wine are woe, sorrow, contention, babbling, wounds, bloodshot eyes, sexual sin, indecent talk, loss of balance and coordination, insensibility, and addiction (Proverbs 23:29-35). Lovers of wine will not be rich (Proverbs 21:17).

Throughout the Old Testament, all who were separated to God were forbidden to drink wine and strong drink. Nazarites were prohibited from drinking alcoholic beverages (Numbers 6:3; Judges 13:7). John the Baptist did not drink it (Luke 1:15). It was not for kings and princes lest it cause them to forget God's law and pervert justice (Proverbs 31:4-5). Priests were forbidden to drink it when they ministered before God in the Tabernacle or Temple (Leviticus 10:9; Ezekiel 44:21).

As Christians, all of us are separated unto God. We are kings and priests, a royal priesthood, and living sacrifices unto God (Revelation 1:6; I Peter 2:9; Romans 12:1). Our special identity indicates that we should not drink alcoholic beverages.

Sin resulted from the first wine drinking recorded in the Bible. When Noah became drunk, he dishonored his own body, causing embarrassment to others and an opportunity for others to sin (Genesis 9:20-25). When Lot became intoxicated, he committed incest with his own daughters (Genesis 19:32-38). God pronounced a woe on drunkenness (Isaiah 5:11). Strong drink caused the people, the priests, and the prophets to err, to lose the way, and to lose their spiritual eyesight (Isaiah 28:7). Wine enslaves the heart of people, just as harlotry does (Hosea 4:11). God also pronounced a woe on those who give drink to their neighbors (Habakkuk 2:15).

The New Testament classifies drunkenness as a sin that will keep people from inheriting the kingdom of God (I Corinthians 6:10; Galatians 5:19-21). Jesus, Paul, and Peter all warned against drunkenness (Luke 21:34; Romans 13:13; Ephesians 5:18; I Peter 4:3). Bishops, deacons, and aged women are specifically instructed not to be given to wine (I Timothy 3:3, 8; Titus 1:7; 2:3).

After reviewing the teaching of Scripture, we conclude that Christians should not indulge in alcoholic beverages. Some biblical references seem to support the drinking of wine, however. To study them, we will investigate the Hebrew and Greek words for wine.

Two major Hebrew words are translated "wine" in the Old Testament. Nine other Hebrew words for various types of wine and strong drink appear only a few times. *Yayin* is the most common word. It can mean any type of wine, but it usually refers to fermented wine. Many verses clearly use *yayin* to mean fermented wine (Genesis 9:21; 19:32; II Samuel 13:28; Esther 1:10; Proverbs 20:1; 23:31; 31:4). *Yayin* can also refer to freshly made, unfermented grape juice (Isaiah 16:10; Jeremiah 48:33).

The other frequently used Hebrew word for wine is

tiyrosh. It almost always refers to newly made, unfermented wine. Only this word is used for the wine that was to be tithed, because God wanted tithes first, before significant fermentation took place (Deuteronomy 12:17; 14:23; Nehemiah 13:5). It is the word used for prosperity in the phrase "corn and wine" (Genesis 27:28, 37; Deuteronomy 7:13; etc.). It is translated "new wine" in many places (Proverbs 3:10; Joel 1:10; etc.) and as "sweet wine" in one place (Micah 6:15). Isaiah 65:8 uses *tiyrosh* to speak of "new wine found in the cluster." Here it clearly refers to unfermented grape juice, even juice still in the grape.

The Greek *oinos* is the original word for wine in the New Testament. It usually refers to fermented wine, but like its Hebrew counterparts it can refer to unfermented wine as well. At least three New Testament verses definitely use it in this way (Matthew 9:17; Mark 2:22; Luke 5:37). These verses say that new, unfermented wine is not placed in old wineskins because when the wine ferments it would burst them. The Greek word *gleukos* appears only once, where it is translated "new wine" (Acts 2:13). It can mean freshly made wine (grape juice), or it can mean sweet wine. The latter could be quite intoxicating, as Acts 2 indicates.

In sum, the word *wine* in both testaments can refer to fermented or unfermented grape juice. In New Testament days, wine was often served at meals, but in this case it was greatly diluted with water so that it would not be intoxicating in normal quantities. Moreover, methods of preserving grape juice in an unfermented condition were well known. In light of these facts and in light of the biblical warnings against wine, we should not use biblical references for wine to promote the drinking of strong alcoholic beverages.

People in the Old Testament often drank alcoholic beverages, but we see the detrimental results. They did not have the overcoming power that accompanies the indwelling Holy Spirit. The law showed people how sinful they were but did not give them power over sin. If it had been perfect, there would be no need for the new covenant. Today, God gives us grace and power to overcome. We can and must live up to God's ideal for the church as a body of separated, holy people.

Jesus turned water into wine at a wedding feast in Cana (John 2:1-11). He thereby performed an act of creation, which indicates that the wine was fresh, not fermented, for fermentation is a process of decay. Verse 10 does not say that the guests got drunk but simply that they had freely drunk the other wine provided by the host. In any case, it is not reasonable to suppose that Jesus gave people a strong drink that would enable them to get drunk. Drunkenness is a sin, and God tempts no one to sin (Galatians 5:21; James 1:13).

Paul advised Timothy, "Drink no longer water, but use a little wine for thy stomach's sake and thine often infirmities" (I Timothy 5:23). He recommended that Timothy drink juice instead of water in order to strengthen his body and soothe his weak stomach. Perhaps he was advising Timothy to stay away from the unsanitary local water or to take a small amount of wine for medicinal purposes. He would not have instructed Timothy to drink a strong alcoholic beverage, for that would only aggravate his weakened condition.

The Bible does not say that Jesus and the disciples

used "wine" at the Last Supper, but it simply says "the fruit of the vine" (Matthew 26:29; Mark 14:25; Luke 22:18). These words tell us that they used juice from the grape without specifying whether it was fermented or not. If it was the typical diluted juice served at meals, then it was not intoxicating. Technically, fresh juice begins to ferment as soon as it is made, unless the process is halted artificially, but in the early stages it is not intoxicating.

Moreover, the same reasons why they used unleavened bread could have led them to use unfermented wine. In this context, leaven symbolizes impurity or sin. Leaven is an agent such as yeast (a type of fungus) that causes the fermentation of bread dough. Chemically, this process is the same type of decay or organic change that causes juice to ferment. The purpose of our discussion is not to prescribe a certain form for the communion service but to show that we cannot use the Last Supper to justify social drinking of alcoholic beverages.

Some Corinthians got drunk at church when partaking of their fellowship meal before the actual communion service (I Corinthians 11:20-22). Each person brought his or her own food (verse 21), and some evidently brought fermented wine. This passage does not condone the practice but condemns it.

In sum, drunkenness is a work of the flesh that will keep people from inheriting the kingdom of God. In addition, both in the Bible and in our day alcohol is the source of many evils. It causes poverty, sickness, lost time, lost money, heartache, violence, evil thoughts, family breakups, sexual sins, physical injuries, mental injuries, and death.

Alcohol is responsible for 4 percent of worldwide disease. According to the World Health Organization, about 1.8 million people die each year due to alcohol consumption. In the U.S., about 75,000 people die each year due to alcohol consumption.[1] Alcohol is a major factor in many other deaths, including 40 percent of traffic fatalities, as well as a factor in 40 percent of all violent crimes.[2] It causes or contributes to a number of diseases such as birth defects (including mental retardation), cirrhosis of the liver, brain damage, and cancer of the mouth, pharynx, larynx, esophagus, liver, and lung. The economic costs of alcohol abuse are estimated to be $185 billion per year in the U.S.[3]

There is no way to measure the sin that alcohol induces, but we can see its effects every day. Surely, these evils are great enough to demonstrate that the warnings of Proverbs 23:29-35 and 21:17 are true.

Even one drink can lower inhibitions, dull the conscience, and impair spiritual discernment. According to a University of Washington study, even a single strong drink can "impair the drinker's driving abilities"; "even a mild dose of alcohol compromises our ability" to take in some information.[4] If this is true with natural faculties, it is also true with spiritual faculties.

The biblical and social arguments for abstention from alcoholic beverages are strong. First, it is practically impossible for people to drink so little that they are never affected mentally or never get drunk. Inevitably, their behavior and actions will be affected to some degree. At that point, they are no longer in complete control of themselves and will often do things they should not do. They are no longer able to fully guard themselves against temptation and sin. They become the servant of alcohol when they yield their bodies to it. Since our bodies are the temple of the Holy Spirit, we do not want anything else to gain control of them. Likewise, we do not want to use something that is physically dangerous and debilitating. Either way, we would defile our bodies.

Second, not everyone can resist the temptation presented by a drink, and not everyone can handle even a small amount of alcohol. The safest course is not to touch it at all. Even those who think they can safely handle it can easily create a stumbling block for others. This is a sufficient reason in itself for abstention according to Romans 14:21. Children and teenagers, as well adults who have struggled with alcohol, all benefit from a good example and are harmed by a bad example.

Finally, the Bible tells us to avoid all appearance of evil (I Thessalonians 5:22). We need to consider our reputation within the church and the reputation of the church in the eyes of the world. To some, abstention may seem extreme, but it is a guaranteed solution to all the problems caused by alcohol. Without the Holy Spirit, abstention may seem difficult or impossible, but the Spirit gives us power to overcome. God makes us a new creation with new loves and desires (II Corinthians 5:17). He takes away the very desire so that we no longer want to drink. The Spirit gives us all the joy, peace, relaxation, and satisfaction that we need (Romans 14:17; Ephesians 5:18). Alcohol may give temporary joy and temporary escape from problems, but the Holy Spirit gives us permanent joy and permanent solutions to our problems.

Drugs and narcotics. Our discussion of the evils of alcohol applies to other drugs as well, for alcohol is a type of drug. Marijuana, for example, causes many of the same evils as alcohol. Its use causes lack of self-control, can cause psychological addiction, and can lead to use of hard drugs. The hard drugs are clearly addictive and physically harmful, and are a major cause of crime. Any recreational drug use that causes the equivalent of drunkenness (loss of self-control), leads to sin, causes physical harm, or causes us to become dependent on it (addiction) is contrary to the will of God. We also need to be cautious with legal medications so as to minimize or avoid these dangers. We should practice moderation, self-control, and self-discipline if we use painkillers, sleeping pills, or other medications.

Tobacco defiles the human body. "To defile" means to dirty, make filthy, dishonor, corrupt the purity or perfection of, contaminate. For centuries, godly leaders have recognized that smoking is filthy and harmful to the body. The Holy Spirit taught them that it was harmful long before science did.

The Bible does not directly refer to tobacco since it was not used in Bible days. It was first used by Native Americans and came to the attention of the world after Europeans discovered America. But the principles of God's Word apply to every age, culture, and country, including circumstances that did not exist in New Testament times. When facing new situations, God leads the church by His Spirit and enables the church to make appropriate decisions and applications of biblical principles. (See Matthew 18:18; Acts 15:28.) Thus, the church body and godly leaders have authority to instruct believers with regard to tobacco and drugs, even though the Bible does not specifically mention them.

Modern science has determined that tobacco is highly

addictive and that smoking is harmful to the body. Consequently, U.S. law currently bans cigarette advertising on television. Every package of cigarettes and every printed advertisement for cigarettes must have a message such as the following: "Warning: The Surgeon General Has Determined That Cigarette Smoking Is Dangerous to Your Health." Smoking is the leading cause of lung cancer and emphysema. It is also associated with many other types of cancer and respiratory illnesses as well as strokes and heart trouble. "Tobacco use is the leading preventable cause of death in the United States, resulting in approximately 440,000 deaths each year. More than 8.6 million people in the United States have at least one serious illness caused by smoking."[5]

According to the World Health Organization, smoking is the second major cause of death worldwide. Ten percent of all adult deaths are now caused by tobacco. If current smoking patterns continue, one-half of the people who smoke—about 650 million people in 2006—will eventually die because of tobacco.[6] Tobacco is responsible for 4.1 percent of worldwide disease.[7]

In addition, tobacco is highly addictive. Many people try to break the habit but simply cannot without God's help. For all these reasons we do not use tobacco in any form.

Conclusion. "Let us cleanse ourselves from all filthiness of the flesh and spirit" (II Corinthians 7:1). "Present your bodies a living sacrifice, holy, acceptable unto God, which is your reasonable service" (Romans 12:1).

Notes

[1]"News Briefs," *Freedomline* (Spirit of Freedom) March-April 2006, 4, citing R. Room, in *The Lancet*, 5 February 2005; Robert Brewer, National Center for Chronic Disease Prevention and Health Promotion; Henry Wechsler, "College Drinking Study," Harvard School of Public Health.

[2]U.S. Department of Justice, *Report on Alcohol and Crime*, 1998, online: http://alcoholism.about.com.

[3]U.S. Department of Health and Human Services, National Institute on Alcohol Abuse and Alcoholism, *Updating Estimates of the Economic Costs of Alcohol Abuse in the United States*, 2000, online: http://pubs.niaaa.nih.gov/publications/economic-2000.

[4]"Study: Even one drink can be dangerous," United Press International, 30 June 2006, online: http://upi.com/NewsTrack.

[5]U.S. Department of Health and Human Services, Centers for Disease Control and Prevention, *Targeting Tobacco Use: The Nation's Leading Cause of Death 2006*, 2, online: http://www.cdc.gov/NCCdphp/publications/aag/pdf/aag_osh2006.pdf.

[6]"Datebook," *U.S. News & World Report*, 5 June 2006, 20.

[7]*Freedomline*, March-April 2006, 4.

CHAPTER

9

Sexual Relationships

Thou shalt not commit adultery (Exodus 20:14).

Abstain from . . . fornication (Acts 15:20).

The Bible is clear in its teaching regarding marriage and sexual relationships. It endorses the marriage of one man and one woman who make a lifelong commitment, and it condemns all sexual relationships outside such a marriage. Numerous passages in both testaments condemn adultery and fornication. Together, these words refer to all extramarital sexual relationships.

Marriage. God instituted marriage in the very beginning by creating Adam and then creating Eve as "a helper comparable to him" (Genesis 2:18, 24, NKJV), or "a helper as his partner" (NRSV). God's purpose in ordaining marriage was to provide for companionship, communion, and partnership between husband and wife and to devise a method of procreation. His plan was for husband and wife to leave their families and form a union with each other (Genesis 2:24). This union was to be heterosexual, lifelong, and monogamous; for God had joined them together.

Although some prominent men in the Old Testament practiced polygamy, this was not God's plan from the beginning. Polygamy was introduced by Lamech, who was also the second recorded murderer (Genesis 4:19, 23). The Bible specifically insists on monogamy for kings, bishops, deacons, and elders (Deuteronomy 17:17; I Timothy 3:2, 12; Titus 1:6).

God hates divorce (Malachi 2:15-16). In Matthew 19:3-9, some Pharisees tested Jesus by asking Him about divorce. He explained that the law of Moses allowed divorce only because of the hardness of people's hearts. Then He reiterated God's original plan for marriage: "They twain shall be one flesh. . . . What therefore God hath joined together, let not man put asunder."

God created sex as a sacred part of the marriage relationship. He is the one who created male and female and placed an attraction between them. Some traditions teach that sex is somehow degrading, carnal, or base. They regard it as an evil necessary for the propagation of the human race, but it is not supposed to be pleasurable, and holy people are not supposed to indulge in it. This view is simply false. Sexual desire within marriage is proper. The purpose of the sexual relationship is for the consummation and strengthening of the union of a man and a woman, as well as for procreation. (See Proverbs 5:15-23; I Corinthians 7:1-5.) Those who forbid marriage are teaching false doctrine (I Timothy 4:1-3). Hebrews

13:4 summarizes the truth about the sexual relationship: "Marriage is honourable in all, and the bed undefiled: but whoremongers and adulterers God will judge."

Because most people in our society, including youth, have been exposed to explicit discussions of sexuality, we must be plain in presenting a biblical viewpoint. Within marriage, the ultimate form of sexual satisfaction as planned by God is sexual intercourse. Various aspects of foreplay and mutual stimulation are also acceptable if both marriage partners agree and find mutual enjoyment. (See Song of Solomon 7:1-13; 8:3.) A couple should not do anything that either considers to be unnatural, unclean, or degrading. (As a possible example, see Leviticus 20:18; Ezekiel 18:6; 22:10.)

Under the law of Moses, various sexual transgressions were punished by death, demonstrating the seriousness with which God views such sins. Although every sin is dangerous and will result in eternal judgment, there is still something particularly serious about sexual sins. The reason is that they violate the sacredness of marriage. Those who commit fornication are joined together as one flesh—a physical, emotional, and spiritual union that God intends to occur only in the context of a lifelong marriage relationship (I Corinthians 6:15-16). Other sins are committed outside the body, but fornication is a sin against one's own body (verse 18).

Sex and marriage are sacred because they involve the lifelong union of two people and because they involve procreation. By the union of male and female, a child is born. This child is a joint creation with God, a soul that will live forever. God intends for a child to be born only within the protected environment of marriage.

Unlike some other sins, once a sexual sin is committed there is no way to make full restitution or put the sinners back into their original status. Thieves may be able to return what they have stolen. Liars may be able to correct their lies. A sexual sin cannot be undone, and it can affect a person for life. Ministers can become disqualified from their position, because they must be blameless, the husband of one wife, and of good report (I Timothy 3:2, 7; Titus 1:6). (See also Luke 9:62.) God will readily forgive those who repent of sexual sins, but these sins often cause serious and even irreversible consequences in this life.

The first general conference of the New Testament church accepted the Old Testament definition and prohibition of sexual sin. It seemed good to the Holy Spirit and to the church to identify the teaching against all forms of sexual immorality as one of the four necessary parts of the Jewish law that all Christians, including Gentiles, must continue to obey (Acts 15:19-29; 21:25).

"Put to death your members which are on the earth: fornication, uncleanness, passion, evil desire, and covetousness, which is idolatry. Because of these things the wrath of God is coming upon the sons of disobedience" (Colossians 3:5-6, NKJV). "For this is the will of God, your sanctification: that you should abstain from sexual immorality; that each of you should know how to possess his own vessel [body—NIV] in sanctification and honor, not in passion of lust, like the Gentiles who do not know God; that no one should take advantage of and defraud his brother in this matter, because the Lord is the avenger of all such, as we also forewarned you and testified. For God did not call us to uncleanness, but in holiness. Therefore he who rejects this does not reject man, but God, who has also given us His Holy Spirit" (I Thessalonians 4:3-8, NKJV).

Let us identify various sexual sins that the Bible condemns.

Fornication, from the Greek *porneia*, means unlawful sexual intercourse or "sexual immorality" (NKJV). Due to the open sinfulness of our day, we must explain plainly that fornication means all sexual intercourse outside a biblical marriage, including oral and anal sex. The Bible recommends marriage as a way to avoid the temptation of fornication (I Corinthians 7:2). Many times the New Testament teaches against fornication. (See I Corinthians 6:13-18; Galatians 5:19; Ephesians 5:3; Colossians 3:5; I Thessalonians 4:3.) In English, when the word *fornication* is used in a restricted sense, it refers to sex involving unmarried people. The law gave the death penalty for this sin (Deuteronomy 22:20-21).

Adultery is prohibited by many passages of Scripture. (See Exodus 20:14; Leviticus 18:20; Deuteronomy 5:18.) Death was the penalty under the law for both parties in a case of adultery with a married woman (Leviticus 20:10; Deuteronomy 22:22). The word refers to sex where at least one party is married, but not to the other. Adultery appears in the lists of the sins of the flesh (Matthew 15:19-20; I Corinthians 6:9-11; Galatians 5:19-21).

Incest is sex between closely related people, such as between parent and child or between siblings. There were twenty laws defining this sin (Leviticus 18:6-18; Deuteronomy 22:30). A man who committed adultery with his father's wife was punished by death (Leviticus 20:11). This sin was present in the Corinthian church and needed to be judged (I Corinthians 5).

Child molestation clearly violates the foregoing teachings against fornication and adultery, and it often involves incest. Abuse of children will result in harsh judgment from God. (See Matthew 18:1-4; Luke 17:2.)

Bestiality, sex with animals, was punished by death for both the person and the animal involved (Exodus 22:19; Leviticus 18:23; 20:15-16; Deuteronomy 27:21).

Rape was punished by death (Deuteronomy 22:23-27).

Lust. Jesus taught, "Whosoever looketh on a woman to lust after her hath committed adultery with her already in his heart" (Matthew 5:28). Temptation that comes to the mind or eye is not sin in itself, but it becomes sin if we entertain it and allow it to develop into lust (James 1:14-15; Matthew 4:1-11). Based on the words of Jesus, if we look at someone who is not our spouse and begin fantasizing about or desiring sex with that person, we have committed sin.

Lewdness and uncleanness. In the biblical teaching against unlawful sexual lust and acts, the KJV uses several additional words: *concupiscence* (strong desire, especially sexual desire), *lasciviousness* ("lewdness" in NKJV), and *uncleanness* (impurity). (See Mark 7:22; II Corinthians 12:21; Galatians 5:19; Colossians 3:5; I Thessalonians 4:3-7.) The latter two words include lustful thoughts, speech, and actions. *Lewdness* refers to anything that promotes or gratifies sexual lust, whether or not a sexual act is committed. *Uncleanness* covers all sexual sin, and it includes perversion (Romans 1:24).

Lascivious or lewd activities include mutual sexual stimulation outside marriage, pornography, voyeurism, exhibitionism, and indecent exposure. Worldly places with a lustful atmosphere and worldly activities that arouse lust fall under this category. Books, music, movies, television, dancing, stories, and jokes can all be lewd.

Intimate embracing can be sexually arousing. Such activity between unmarried persons leads to lust and often to fornication. Thus, holding hands, hugging, and kissing are not appropriate for casual dating but should be reserved for serious relationships and should be carefully controlled. Any further intimacy must be reserved for marriage. It is wrong for unmarried couples to engage in intimate caressing or other sexual stimulation. Even between engaged couples, kissing and embracing should be controlled.

Pornography is a serious problem in our day, especially since it is readily available on the Internet, cable television, videos, and DVDs, as well as in print. It is strongly addictive. To avoid this sin, it is important to place controls on these media and to maintain spiritual disciplines such as prayer, fasting, and Bible study. In addition, to overcome this sin, it is also important to become accountable to one's spouse and possibly to a mentor or prayer partner. The pastor can help to implement an appropriate system of accountability, control, and spiritual discipline.

Overcoming lust. In *Every Man's Battle*, Stephen Arterburn et al. offer practical recommendations for overcoming sexual lust, which we summarize below:[1]

- Identify times and occasions of weakness and develop strategies for avoiding them. [Temptations are often strongest when men are hungry, angry, lonely, or tired—HALT.]

- Bounce the eyes: In a tempting situation, immediately look away.
- Starve the eyes: Deprive the eyes of sexual gratification that comes from outside marriage.
- Sword and shield: Use Bible verses to attack (Job 31:1) and defend (I Corinthians 6:18-20).
- Victory in your mind: Take control of thoughts (II Corinthians 10:5) and think rationally.
- Victory in your heart: Cherish your wife, honor your wife, and keep your commitments.

Archibald Hart offers similar advice in *The Sexual Man*, as summarized below:[2]

- Own up to your lust and admit it is a problem that needs to be controlled. Don't excuse it. Don't rationalize it away. Just be honest with yourself.
- Don't feed your lust. Cut out anything in your life that feeds it. Don't dwell on thoughts that foster it. Dispose of all sources of stimulation that provoke your lustfulness.
- Develop alternative diversionary strategies. Find a hobby or activity that you can turn to whenever your feelings of lust become overwhelming.
- Change your beliefs about sexual lust. Remind yourself that pictures are only pictures, not people, and that you don't have a right to take anyone you desire to bed with you in your imagination.
- Observe how others who have allowed their lust to go too far have fallen and learn your lesson from their failures, not your own. Prevention is better than cure.
- Try to find the underlying reason for your lust,

beyond just blaming it on your strong sex drive. Lots of men have a strong drive, but are not dominated by lust. Were you love-deprived as a child? Sexually abused? Getting these repressed reasons out into the light can help free you from their hidden power.

- If you cannot bring lust under control by yourself, get help.

In all situations that could involve fornication, lewdness, uncleanness, or pornography, we should take our thoughts and temptations to God. We can cast down imaginations and bring into captivity every thought to the obedience of Christ (II Corinthians 10:5). Instead of limiting God's power, let us trust Him for the strength to resist temptation and be holy in our thoughts as well as actions.

Masturbation (self-stimulation). The Bible does not say anything about masturbation, so we will look to general scriptural teachings on sexual matters. We can identify two potential problems: lustful fantasies and addictive behavior. Ultimately, this is a question that each individual will have to answer personally.

Jesus taught that if a man looks at a woman lustfully he has committed adultery with her in his heart (Matthew 5:28). Paul advised Timothy to flee youthful lusts, to keep a good conscience, and to keep a pure heart (I Timothy 1:19; II Timothy 2:22). Lustful, lascivious thoughts are contrary to the Word of God. At the least, fantasizing about sexual relationships with a particular individual other than one's spouse is contrary to the teachings of the Bible. Questions to ask are: Does masturbation lead one to entertain improper lusts and fantasies? Does masturbation make one feel guilty or defiled?

Another point to consider is the purpose of sex. God designed it to be an important component of the intimate personal relationship between husband and wife. Sex is meant to be a shared expression of joy and love. Thus, it seems that habitual masturbation or psychological dependence on masturbation is not God's plan.

Effeminate behavior is a sin that will keep men from inheriting the kingdom of God (I Corinthians 6:9-10). The KJV word is from the Greek *malakos*, which means "soft, i.e. fine (clothing), figuratively a catamite."[3] A catamite is a boy kept for purposes of sexual perversion. In other contexts, this word is translated as "soft," for soft raiment or clothing (Matthew 11:8; Luke 7:25). The same passage also lists "abusers of themselves with mankind" (Greek, *arsenokoitēs*). The NKJV translates these two words as "homosexuals" and "sodomites," which are synonymous in English. The *Interlinear Greek-English New Testament* translates the first as "voluptuous persons" and the second as "sodomites."

The primary reference is to homosexual activity, but the use of two words instead of merely one is significant. Some scholars suggest that the intent is to encompass both the passive partner and the active partner in homosexual relationships. We conclude that these words prohibit all homosexual behavior as well as men looking, acting, or dressing like women.

In this regard, we note that Deuteronomy 22:5 prohibits both males and females from wearing clothing that pertains to the opposite sex, which in its most blatant form is called *transvestism*. (See chapter 6.) Similarly, men are to have short hair, while women are to have long hair (I Corinthians 11:14-15). (See chapter 7.) Clearly,

God intends for there to be a clear distinction between the sexes. Men should not be effeminate and women should not be mannish in mannerisms, behavior, or dress.

Homosexual behavior, or sexual relations between people of the same sex, will prevent someone from inheriting the kingdom of God (I Corinthians 6:9-10). When it involves women, this sin is also called *lesbianism*. The law gave the death penalty for homosexual acts (Leviticus 20:13). These acts are an abomination—something that will keep people from heaven (Leviticus 18:22; Revelation 21:27). Both prostitution and sodomy were so abhorrent that the money obtained by such activities could not be brought to the house of God (Deuteronomy 23:17-18). The price charged by a male prostitute was called the "hire of a dog" and was forbidden as an offering.

Homosexuality is called *sodomy* from the story of Sodom in Genesis 19:4-11. When two angels in the form of men visited Lot's house, the men of Sodom attempted to assault them sexually. They asked Lot to bring his guests out "that we may know them"—a biblical euphemism for sexual intercourse. (See Genesis 4:1.) When Lot refused, they threatened to do worse to him than to his visitors. They refused to take Lot's two virgin daughters instead of the angels. Finally, the angels pulled Lot into the house, shut the door, and struck the men with blindness. Even then, the men "wearied themselves to find the door."

Homosexuality is one of the major sins for which God destroyed the city. Some people claim that the men's sin was only their inhospitality rather than their homosexuality. Jude 7 refutes this notion, saying the people of Sodom sinned by giving themselves to sexual immorality and "going after strange flesh." (See also II Peter 2:6-22.)

A similar story occurs in Judges 19:22-25. Certain men of Gibeah in Benjamin, whom the Bible calls "sons of Belial," tried to assault a male guest in the town. They were appeased only when he allowed them to have his concubine, whom they raped until she died. The other tribes demanded that these men be executed, but the Benjamites protected them. A civil war resulted that almost completely destroyed the tribe of Benjamin.

Another Old Testament story shows that it is important to guard against the possibility of homosexual misconduct. Noah got drunk on wine one day and lay naked in his tent in a drunken sleep (Genesis 9:20-27). One of his sons, Ham, observed Noah's nakedness and told his brothers. The brothers, Shem and Japheth, went in backwards and covered their father. When Noah awoke, he "knew what his younger son had done unto him." He pronounced a curse on Ham, saying that Ham's offspring would be a servant of Shem and Japheth. The wording and the magnitude of the punishment indicate that Ham's transgression was serious—possibly involving homosexual lust or action.

Kings Asa, Jehoshaphat, and Josiah removed sodomites from the land of Judah in accordance with God's will and as a part of their reform programs (I Kings 15:12; 22:46; II Kings 23:7). One of Judah's great sins was allowing boys to be sold as prostitutes (Joel 3:3). Pagan religions of that day incorporated homosexuality and female prostitution in ritual worship. Some have argued that this was the only reason why the Old Testament condemns homosexuality, but this argument cannot account for the judgment upon Sodom or the strong teachings of the New Testament.

The New Testament church endorsed the Old Testament teaching against homosexuality when it announced that Christians must abstain from fornication, that is, all sexual transgressions as defined by the law of Moses (Acts 15:19-29).

Romans 1 includes homosexual conduct in its account of the step-by-step decline of the human race into sin. It states that all humans have an opportunity to know the existence and power of God. Therefore, they are without excuse if they refuse to acknowledge and worship Him (verse 20). Since they did not glorify Him as God, nor were they thankful, they began to worship images of His creation instead of Him (verses 21-23). As a result, God gave them up to uncleanness "to dishonour their own bodies between themselves" (verse 24). Since they worshiped the creature more than the Creator, God gave them up to "vile affections." The women changed the natural use of their bodies into something that is against nature, namely, lesbianism (verse 26). Likewise, the men left the natural use of the woman and burned in lust towards each other, "men with men working that which is unseemly" (verse 27). They did not like to retain the knowledge of God, so God gave them over to a reprobate (debased, depraved) mind (verse 28).

Homosexuality is contrary to nature, because it involves use of the body contrary to God's design. It thwarts God's purpose for instituting sexuality, namely, to operate in the context of marriage between a man and a woman. In that setting, sex is a strong bond that unites male and female in a complementary relationship, and it provides the means for procreation. Homosexuality does not advance either purpose.

Some apologists claim that homosexuality is natural because researchers have occasionally observed this behavior among animals. At most, this evidence would show that such behavior is bestial or animalistic, not a model for humans. We do not think that other common animal behaviors such as forced sexual intercourse, violent aggression, unprovoked killing, and cannibalism are appropriate for humans.

Romans 1 reveals that homosexuality is the final depravity that results when humans persistently refuse to worship God. It is the final outcome of worshiping the creation—that is, the body—instead of God.

This passage does not say that an individual who practices homosexuality is necessarily a greater sinner than others, however. Rather, it indicates that as human society moves further and further away from godly principles, there will be a greater incidence of homosexuality. It becomes more prevalent as society gets further from God, as homes and marriages break up, as men abdicate their responsibilities, as women usurp the male role, and as evil spirits are able to operate more freely. Homosexuality is not necessarily a sign of extraordinary individual sin, but it is a product and a sign of the evil age in which we live.

No one who practices homosexuality can inherit the kingdom of God (I Corinthians 6:9-10). As previously discussed, this passage uses two Greek words to define homosexuality—*malakos* and *arsenokoitēs*—which the NKJV translates as "homosexuals" and "sodomites." The word *arsenokoitēs* comes from the word *arsēn*, meaning "male, man," and *koitē*, literally meaning "bed" and by extension "sexual intercourse." This language is as clear and unambiguous as possible.

We find another condemnation of homosexuality in I Timothy 1:10 using the same Greek word, which is translated as "them that defile themselves with mankind" (KJV) or "sodomites" (NKJV).

In the Tribulation, Jerusalem will be called the city of Sodom and Egypt (Revelation 11:8). In other words, it will be the headquarters of sexual perversion and spiritual adultery.

The word *uncleanness* includes all types of immorality, perversion, and homosexuality as in Romans 1:24. The New Testament repeatedly condemns uncleanness. (See II Corinthians 12:21; Galatians 5:19; Ephesians 4:19; 5:3; Colossians 3:5; I Thessalonians 4:7; II Peter 2:10.)

Our study reveals that homosexual behavior is sinful. It is not an illness or an alternative lifestyle, although typically it becomes an addiction or a spiritual bondage. To those who repent and seek deliverance, God will give power to resist temptation and live a new life.

Likewise, *transgender* or *transsexual* behavior is sinful. These terms refer to people who live contrary to their biological sex or undergo a sex-change operation. When such people repent, they should seek ways to fulfill God's original plan for their lives once again. If this proves to be impossible, they can live in celibacy. (Perhaps the principle of I Corinthians 7:20-24 would apply here. See NKJV.)

Factors that influence homosexual behavior. Certain factors can increase a person's susceptibility to homosexual temptations. Some characteristics of culture, personality, physique, background, or life experience can make a person vulnerable, just as some people are prone to alcoholism, promiscuity, or criminal conduct. But by

God's grace, these factors can be overcome.

Science has not demonstrated that homosexuality is genetic in origin. It is not correct to say, "I was born a homosexual," or "God made me a homosexual." Homosexuality cannot be strictly hereditary, for throughout history those who were exclusively homosexual could not procreate and therefore could not pass on their genes to future generations. A few homosexual researchers have claimed to find features of brain structure or chemistry that they link to homosexuality, but if these characteristics indeed exist, they are most likely a result of homosexual activity rather than a cause. In the final analysis, if there were some biological component to homosexuality, it would simply demonstrate that human nature has been corrupted by sin, just as the Bible teaches.

In reality, conscious human behavior involves a complex interplay of biological, environmental, and psychological factors. Humans are not creatures of instinct, but they have the power to choose and regulate their conduct. While we cannot escape the power of sin except by God's grace, we can choose to act or refrain from acting in specific ways. If this were not so, there would be no point in outlawing various forms of criminal behavior.

It is true that some people become aware of homosexual thoughts and tendencies at an early age and do not remember a time when they consciously chose homosexuality over heterosexuality. Their thoughts and feelings were molded by factors early in life. It is helpful to identify such factors in order to help prevent and overcome homosexuality, but they do not provide any justification for continuing in this lifestyle.

As is true of other sinful behavior, most societies have

some incidence of homosexuality. Overall, lesbianism is rare, and the exclusive, lifelong practice of homosexuality is practically nonexistent. Many homosexuals are actually bisexual in practice, and most have had some heterosexual experience. Relatively few enter into a lifelong, monogamous, homosexual relationship. Indeed, most homosexuals are quite promiscuous.

Psychologists have identified a number of factors that help to shape homosexual behavior. Children are more likely to become homosexual if they are not able to identify with their same-sex parent but become excessively attached to the opposite-sex parent. For example, if a father is physically absent from the home, is grossly abusive, is ineffectual and weak, or is feared and hated, there is a greater chance that his son will identify with his mother. The same thing can happen when the mother is extremely affectionate but controlling or domineering.

In such situations, the boy may identify with the feminine role and may crave male approval and love. He may resent his mother's domination or feel inadequate in comparison to her, and then transfer these feelings to women in general. He may see all women as untouchable saintly figures like his mother. Or he may become so overly loyal to his mother that he cannot have a normal relationship with another woman. Any one of these reactions can lead to homosexuality.

Another key influence is early sexual experience. A childhood or youthful encounter with a homosexual can shape behavior later on, especially if the experience is perceived as normal or pleasurable. Children who are molested by same-sex persons may grow to think of such encounters as normal or to define their identity by such encounters. When youth undergo puberty and begin to develop sexual awareness, they can be strongly influenced by homosexual experimentation or seduction.

An early love affair that ends disastrously, including one that results in an illegitimate child or an abortion, may cause feelings of rejection, guilt, and fear that can push the individual away from the other sex. Feelings of physical inadequacy, sometimes stemming from physical or emotional problems, can do the same. Moreover, adolescent alienation is a powerful force. The lack of suitable same-sex friends and a lack of participation in typical activities of the same sex can create a need for companionship and acceptance that is later met by homosexuality. Alienation and ridicule from peers may also drive the adolescent into contact and relationships with homosexuals, who can easily influence him.

Women who have had abusive relationships with men sometimes retreat into lesbianism. They may feel safer with another woman or may feel that it is easier to understand and be understood by another woman.

When the prevailing culture condones and glamorizes homosexual behavior, it encourages experimentation and involvement. People who are struggling with their identity, people who are rebounding from a bad situation, and people who are jaded by their life of promiscuity can become candidates for the homosexual life. As Romans 1 teaches, when society rejects God, it descends into worship of the creation, which leads to worship of the body, which leads to sexual immorality and promiscuity. Sexual immorality leads to the breakdown of marriage and family. As marriages and families become dysfunctional and disintegrate, the factors that promote homosexuality become more prevalent.

At the same time, people find that sexual immorality does not provide the satisfaction and fulfillment that they expected. Thus, they place even more emphasis on sexuality, become more promiscuous, and seek new forms of immorality, all in a vain attempt to find satisfaction. This quest leads to an increase of all kinds of deviant sexual behavior, including multiple marriages, fetishism, sadism, masochism, hardcore pornography, child molestation, transvestism, bestiality, and homosexuality. Thus, the widespread practice and acceptance of homosexuality indicates that society has reached the final stage of degeneration from God's plan, just as Romans 1 explains. We have arrived at this point in twenty-first-century Western culture.

An understanding of these influences and processes can help leaders to prevent, correct, or at least counteract unhealthy situations. This understanding also helps people who are struggling with homosexual desires by showing them some of the contributing factors. Once they realize that they were not born a certain way but have been influenced by unhealthy relationships and negative events, they have hope for change. They can take responsibility for their actions and can begin to remold their lives. They can learn how to modify their thinking, habits, and behavior and, most of all, how to trust God for victory.

An understanding of these matters can also help parents to raise their children properly. For instance, we see how important it is for fathers to develop warm personal relationships with their children; for wives not to usurp their husbands' authority in the home; for children to have suitable same-sex companionship with their peers; and for parents, especially mothers, not to pamper, over-indulge, or overprotect their sons.

We also realize that we cannot trust society or public schools to offer appropriate guidance in sexual matters. Instead, parents and churches must provide the necessary training in biblical truth, including the different roles of the sexes and the proper relationship between the sexes. We must teach our children and youth how to avoid unhealthy situations and how to deal with problems. We must protect them from unwholesome influences and experiences that can influence them in the wrong direction at a crucial stage in their lives.

Overcoming homosexual behavior. As we have already stated, psychological and environmental factors do not justify the practice of homosexuality. Every habitual sin can be influenced or encouraged by an unhealthy background and negative experiences. Adults still have the ability and responsibility to determine what is right and wrong and to choose what is right. Many people have overcome under similar circumstances, even those who were subjected to the same family and environment factors. Ultimately, through the Holy Spirit we receive power to be victorious in every situation as we learn to yield to God.

At the same time, we must recognize that homosexuality is a powerful force. First, it typically results from early life experiences that are hard to erase. Second, it has usually developed over a long period of time and has become an ingrained habit. Third, spiritual forces are involved, so that people who want deliverance from homosexual desires need God's help.

While a person can make a decision to stop committing homosexual acts, in most cases deliverance from homosexual desires is a long, difficult process. As with all habitual sins, some people seem to experience a more complete eradication of unwholesome desires than others, but those who are delivered should be careful not to expose themselves to unnecessary temptation. Overcoming is accomplished by consistent prayer, walking in the Spirit, disciplining the mind, and obtaining godly support and counsel. The goal should be complete deliverance, which can be obtained through patience, a determination to overcome, and a total love for God. Psalm 37:4 is literally applicable: "Delight thyself also in the LORD; and he shall give thee the desires of thine heart."

The first step is to cease homosexual activities. The Bible defines homosexuality in terms of practice, so when people stop participating in homosexual acts and stop entertaining homosexual lusts, then they are no longer homosexuals. The next step is to seek deliverance from homosexual desires. The third step is for God to give the normal heterosexual desires that He intends for all to have. Those who have fallen into homosexual sin must not accept homosexuality as a basic part of their personality but must realize that it is a learned (whether consciously or unconsciously) habit that can be eradicated.

We should treat homosexuals like anyone else who needs God—namely, with respect and friendship. We should not look on them with ridicule or contempt, but we should show them Christian love and concern. We do not approve of their conduct, but we accept them as persons. We do not offer condemnation but encouragement and hope. (See John 3:16-17.)

Homosexuals may be sincere, hungry for God, and

of good moral character in many ways. Often they are extremely lonely and desperate. They usually go through an agonizing period of self-hatred, depression, and despondency until their conscience becomes seared. Our challenge is to reach out to them in love and introduce them to the baptism of the Holy Spirit. Through this experience they will receive power to change. There is no need to exclude them from church services unless they try to entice others in the church to participate in their sin. This danger usually arises from people who claim to be Christians but hide their homosexual behavior and secretly try to involve others.

If young men struggle with effeminate tendencies, the pastor, youth pastor, or other approved leader should counsel, guide, and mentor them individually so that they can become more masculine in speech, mannerisms, and dress. In some cases, they simply have lacked appropriate male role models and training. They do not need to be used in leadership unless they make progress in this area. Young women who struggle with masculine tendencies need similar assistance.

At the same time, we need to guard against the spirit of suspicion. A man who seems to have some feminine mannerisms may not be homosexual. Just because he is more sensitive than most men or more talented in certain areas does not mean he is homosexual. Even if someone struggles with homosexual temptations, he should be respected if he resists them and refuses to act on them.

In short, we cannot stereotype people, nor should we assume, insinuate, or charge that someone is guilty of homosexual activity based simply on certain mannerisms. Some very masculine men are homosexual, so appearances can be deceiving. Of course, we should protect our children and youth from unhealthy influences and encounters. Pastors have the responsibility to guard the flock and to warn against sin.

We can overcome all forms of sexual temptation and sin, including homosexual behavior. Inside everyone is a latent desire for the opposite sex if only the layers of habit and experience can be removed. The Holy Spirit will give the power to overcome. Pastor and friends must patiently offer their support, and the person must pray continually. Most importantly, the person must have a sincere determination to change his or her life and a sincere desire to live for God.

Conclusion. Adultery, fornication, lust, lewdness, pornography, and homosexuality are great dangers today, for the prevailing spirits of the world always attack the church. Pastors must teach and preach against these sins. It is advisable to organize men's and women's meetings to address these issues. It is also good to hold meetings for youth to discuss dating, intimate embracing and caressing, fornication, homosexuality, and marriage. Some meetings need to be held separately for males and females with appropriate respective teachers such as the pastor and pastor's wife. We must meet the challenge of the end time in these areas!

Resources to assist in overcoming sexual lust, pornography, sexual addiction, and homosexual behavior are available from Focus on the Family, *www.pureintimacy.org*, and *www.beaconministries.net* (an Apostolic Web site dealing with homosexuality).

There are many cases of overcomers. Paul told the Corinthians, after listing fornicators, adulterers, homosexuals, and other types of sinners, "And such were some of you: but ye are washed, but ye are sanctified, but ye are justified in the name of the Lord Jesus, and by the Spirit of our God" (I Corinthians 6:9-11). We can conquer all sin, including sexual sin, through faith in Jesus Christ, heartfelt repentance, baptism in Jesus' name, the baptism of the Holy Spirit, and daily spiritual disciplines as we rely on the power of the Spirit.

Notes

[1]Stephen Arterburn, Fred Stoeker, and Mike Yorkey, *Every Man's Battle: Winning the War on Sexual Temptation One Victory at a Time* (Colorado Springs: WaterBrook, 2000).

[2]Archibald Hart, *The Sexual Man* (Nashville: Word, 1994).

[3]James Strong, *Exhaustive Concordance of the Bible* (Nashville: Abingdon, 1890).

CHAPTER

10

Abstaining from Bloodshed

Thou shalt not kill (Exodus 20:13).
Do not kill (Mark 10:19).

A basic law. One of God's basic laws is that one person should not take the life of another person. God gave the first law against murder in Genesis 9:5-6, pronouncing judgment on all who deliberately shed human blood. The Ten Commandments include a condemnation of murder (Exodus 20:13). The New Testament reaffirms this emphasis on the sacredness of human life. Numerous passages classify murder as a sin (Matthew 15:19; Mark 7:21; Galatians 5:21).

Murder. Why is it wrong to kill another human being? First, it is a sin against God, who created humans in His own image (Genesis 9:6). It destroys God's image creature. God has a purpose and a plan for each life. Each person is unique and fits into God's plan in a way that no other person can. God desires the special worship that each person gives in his or her unique way. Murder deprives God of the victim's worship and his or her part in God's plan.

Murder is also a sin against family and society. Family, friends, and loved ones are all victimized by the loss of the one who loved and supported them.

Finally, murder is a sin against the victims. It cuts them off from completing their duties to both God and humans. If they are not saved, then they have no further chance to learn about God or to repent of their sins. In this situation, the killer sends the victim into eternity without God. In short, no one has the personal authority to take someone else's life.

The positive teaching is that we should respect all humans and seek to preserve human life. Jesus called us to a high standard of holiness, exceeding that of the Old Testament: "Ye have heard that it hath been said, An eye for an eye, and a tooth for a tooth: But I say unto you, That ye resist not evil: but whosoever shall smite thee on thy right cheek, turn to him the other also. . . . Ye have heard that it hath been said, Thou shalt love thy neighbour, and hate thine enemy. But I say unto you, Love your enemies, bless them that curse you, do good to them that hate you, and pray for them which despitefully use you, and persecute you. . . . Be ye therefore perfect, even as your Father which is in heaven is perfect" (Matthew 5:38-39, 43-44, 48).

Here Jesus taught us to put away violence, animosity, and revenge. Society has a responsibility to maintain order and promote justice. (See Romans 13:1-7.) At the same time, Christians are to act in a kind, loving way toward everyone.

Hatred. "Whosoever hateth his brother is a murderer: and ye know that no murderer hath eternal life abiding in him" (I John 3:15). Not only must we abstain from the physical act of murder, but we must not let hatred lodge in our hearts. Instead, we must resolve conflicts, get rid of grudges, and do what we can to live in peace with others. We must pray until we do not harbor malice or bitterness toward those who have wronged us. We must also oppose any form of hatred or ill will toward groups of people, such as racial prejudice.

Warfare and self-defense. How does the teaching of Jesus apply in times of warfare and self-defense? Society has the right to protect its citizens in these cases. Nevertheless, as Christians we do not want to kill another human being even in these situations. Instead, we pray for God's protection and care. We rely upon God to deliver us from situations where we might feel forced to take another life, and we use prudence to avoid such situations.

In times of war, we can support our nation in a just cause through noncombatant roles and roles that help to preserve life, such as medical personnel, supply personnel, and chaplains. We believe in supporting our country and obeying governmental authority (I Peter 2:13-17).

As Christians, we do not fight for an earthly kingdom (John 18:36). Our warfare is spiritual and not physical (Ephesians 6:12). When Stephen was stoned, he did not throw stones back, but he looked to Jesus and prayed for his murderers (Acts 7:55-60). When Peter tried to defend Jesus with a sword, the Lord rebuked him, "All they that take the sword shall perish with the sword" (Matthew 26:52).

Should Christians carry deadly weapons for self-defense? To answer this question, we should ask, What is my purpose? What would I do if I had a confrontation with someone? Would I try to kill someone? Are there any circumstances in which I would be willing to kill someone? How would I feel if killed someone?

In the Old Testament, Israel engaged in warfare against its enemies, but is this example a model for Christians today? Under the old covenant, God chose the nation of Israel as His witness to the world. Through Israel, He brought forth His Word and ultimately the Savior for the whole world. God gave the Israelites their own land in which they could live as a unique, holy people separated unto Jehovah. They were to be a light to the rest of the world, an example that would show everyone how great the God of Israel was and would encourage all nations to serve Him. Israel did not fulfill this plan completely, yet God still used Israel to bring the Messiah into the world to provide salvation for everyone.

This plan required the preservation of the nation of Israel. Some nations opposed Israel's existence, however, and Israel's worship of Jehovah. They jeopardized God's promises to Israel and His plan of salvation. As a result, God commanded Israel to fight against them. Moreover, the pagans of Canaan had completely rejected God and were living in gross sinfulness. God decided that the time had come to purge the land of their abominations; the time for their judgment had arrived. God used Israel as an instrument for executing that judgment.

Today, God no longer deals primarily with nations but with individuals. The plan of salvation emphasizes individuals. "Whosoever shall call on the name of the Lord shall be saved" (Acts 2:21). God's chosen people are not a physical nation that must fight for its natural existence and identity, but they are individuals chosen out of every nation and spiritually separated from the world.

Moreover, under the law of Moses judgment was swift and strict. Often, sinners were immediately punished by death. Under grace, judgment is deferred and mercy is extended in a much greater measure. God determines judgment on an individual basis; we do not have authority to judge anyone personally (Matthew 7:1).

Finally, under the new covenant, we are called to a higher standard of personal holiness. The words of Jesus urge us to turn away from violence, retaliation, and revenge. Through the baptism of the Holy Spirit we receive power to fulfill this teaching in a way that Old Testament believers could not.

In the second and third centuries, Christians avoided the violence that was so prevalent in pagan society. Roland Bainton, a Yale University historian, stated:

> Gladiatorial combats were condemned and the Christians could not witness them. Christians could assume no magisterial post that carried with it the possibility of passing a sentence of death. . . . Military service was allowed but warfare rejected. This appears in the Canons of Hippolytus who said that a Christian might be a soldier provided he did not kill.[1]

For further discussion of these teachings in church history and today, see David K. Bernard, *Practical Holiness: A Second Look*.

Abortion. Unborn children in the womb of their mothers are humans created in God's image. Therefore, it is a sin to take their lives. (See Genesis 9:5-6.) At conception, the sperm and the ovum unite to form a living, growing organism that science identifies as human. By the third week, the heart begins beating, and the brain begins to send impulses throughout the body.[2] Within a month after conception—that is, by the time the mother knows she is pregnant—it is possible to distinguish the baby's eyes, feet, and head.

Unborn babies are living souls. We cannot identify any time after conception when they suddenly become human or become living souls, yet in the U.S. and most of the world unborn babies can be legally killed in the womb up to the very moment of delivery. If they become souls only after nine months, then what about premature babies? If they become souls only when they leave the womb, what about test-tube babies conceived outside the womb? If they become souls only after viability (when they become able of surviving outside the womb), then what about the medical advances that have dramatically increased the survival rates of babies born extremely premature? Does a baby's humanity depend on the state of available technology?

The Bible indicates that God considers a child in the womb to be a human in every sense of the word. God sanctified, or set apart, Jeremiah for a particular purpose while he was still in his mother's womb (Jeremiah 1:5). David stated that the Lord was his God from his mother's womb (Psalm 22:10). He also acknowledged that he acquired a sinful human nature at conception (Psalm 51:5).

To purposely abort a child means to kill that child. What is the difference between killing a child in the womb and killing a premature baby who is born at the same stage of development? Is one human but not the other? Is one a living soul but not the other? We have no scriptural authority for drawing an arbitrary line after conception. We are playing God if we decide that one is a human being and the other is not, or that one deserves to live and the other does not.

Pregnancy is procreation. It is God's means of creating a new human being in conjunction with the mother and father. Once pregnancy begins, the decision is out of human hands. God's purpose, the sanctity of human life, and the unborn child's right to live take precedence over the wishes and convenience of the parents.

A miscarriage, also called a spontaneous abortion, is nature's way of dealing with a nonviable fetus. A deliberate abortion, however, is human intervention in an attempt to play God.

Contraception (prevention of conception) is acceptable since it does not involve destroying an individual that has already been conceived. After a human being comes into existence, however, the time for deciding whether to have a child has passed.

In cases of imminent danger to the mother's life, a decision can be made to deliver a child early with the goal of preserving both lives if possible. If nothing is done, both mother and child will die, so in this case there is no wrongful intent to kill the baby. At the same time, we should remember that God is a healer. Righteous women should claim God's promise to bring salvation (deliverance, protection) in childbearing. (See I Timothy 2:15.)

Abortion, the Bible, and the Christian by Donald Shoemaker discusses the lack of justification for abortion when there is economic hardship, social hardship, a possibility of mental or physical birth defects, a maternal psychiatric problem, rape, or incest.[3] In the case of rape or incest, it is possible to take some immediate actions to prevent conception.

In sum, we do not have the right to take the life of a defenseless human being because of a mistake made by someone else. Moreover, if abortion were morally justifiable for whatever reasons, what would prevent us from killing the newborn infant, the mentally handicapped, the physically handicapped, the orphan, or the aged for the same reasons?

Suicide is also contrary to the Word of God, as it takes the life of someone who is created in the image of God. No human has the authority to take away the life that God has given him or her. As Christians we should not consider suicide to be an option but a sin. When suicide does take place, however, we should respond pastorally with compassion for the surviving family, recognizing that God is merciful. Perhaps the suicide victim was not in his or her right mind and so would not be fully accountable.

When problems seem to overwhelm us so that suicide might be a temptation, we need to turn to God for strength. The Holy Spirit will give us joy and peace (Romans 14:17; Galatians 5:22). Through prayer, fasting, and faithful endurance we can receive answers to difficult problems. God has promised never to allow us to be tempted beyond what we can bear, and He has promised always to make a way of escape for us (I Corinthians 10:13).

Suicide is an attempt to evade problems and responsibilities, but it actually offers no escape, because everyone will face reality on judgment day. If we do not resolve our problems and temptations in this life, then we will have no other chance to do so, but we will face the consequences in eternity. Suicide does not allow God to work in the situation and does not allow God's purpose to be fulfilled.

Conclusion. God has created every human in His image and has given each one a purpose in life. As Christians, we should not seek to take away a human life that God has granted.

Notes

[1]Roland Bainton, *Early Christianity* (Princeton, NJ: Van Nostrand, 1960), 50, 54.

[2]Gary Bergel with C. Everett Koop, *Abortion in America* and *When You Were Formed in Secret* (Elyria, Ohio: Intercessors for America, 1980).

[3]Donald Shoemaker, *Abortion, the Bible, and the Christian* (Grand Rapids: Baker, 1977).

CHAPTER

11

Honesty and Integrity

Thou shalt not steal (Exodus 20:15).
Do not steal . . . Defraud not (Mark 10:19).

In this chapter we will study various questions related to personal honesty and integrity, namely, theft, fraud, paying taxes, paying debts, extortion, and bribery. (For a discussion of lying, see chapter 4.)

Theft. The Bible teaches respect for the property and possessions of others. Stealing is the act of taking someone's property without his or her consent. Theft is wrong regardless of the value of the stolen goods, the wealth of the victim, or the poverty of the thief. The Bible admonishes, "Let him that stole steal no more: but rather let him labour, working with his hands the thing which is good, that he may have to give to him that needeth" (Ephesians 4:28).

The proper way to obtain what we need is to work

for it. "If any would not work, neither should he eat" (II Thessalonians 3:10). Some believe that if poor people truly need something, they are justified in taking it from a rich person who can easily replace it. Others hold that if something is not guarded, the owners do not consider it to be valuable and so do not deserve to keep it. These are human rationalizations, however, not the Word of God. Neither the old covenant (law of Moses) nor the new covenant (teaching of Jesus) allows such exceptions, but they simply command, "Do not steal."

To be as practical as possible, let us give some examples of stealing:

- *Checking out a book from a library and not returning it.*
- *Downloading copyrighted songs, movies, or books from the Internet without permission or payment.*
- *Making copies of copyrighted software in order for other people to possess it without permission or payment.*
- *Borrowing money without intending or attempting to repay.*
- *Refusing to give tithes and offerings to God* (Malachi 3:8-12). Tithing began before the law, for Abraham and Jacob paid tithes (Genesis 14:20; 28:22). Jesus endorsed the practice (Matthew 23:23), and Paul gave lessons on giving (I Corinthians 9:7-14). Ministers should pay tithes on their income, even if they receive their income from the tithes of others (Nehemiah 10:38; Hebrews 7:9). Many other passages of Scripture teach or com-

mend the paying of tithes. (See Leviticus 27:30; Numbers 18:21; Deuteronomy 14:22; Proverbs 3:9; Luke 11:42; Hebrews 7:5-10.) When we give tithes (ten percent of net income) and offerings (free-will giving of any amount), we honor God as the true owner of everything we possess. He is the one who gives life, health, strength, ability to work, and opportunity to receive income. He is the one who has supplied our needs and blessed us materially. We are stewards of these blessings, and by giving a small portion to His kingdom we acknowledge His ownership and give thanks for His blessings. When we refuse to do so, we actually rob God.

- *Taking supplies or money from an organization without payment or consent of the one in charge.* When people take supplies or money belonging to an organization, they sometimes justify their actions by saying that they belong to the organization and are thereby entitled to use the funds as they wish. For instance, one person misappropriated church funds using the rationale, "This is God's money and I am God's child." This argument ignores the clear distinction between personal and organizational property and the principles of authority that must be followed. The organization's managers are responsible for the proper use of the property. When members of an organization take property for personal use without proper authority, they have stolen from the organization and its managers. They have stolen from the group of people who donated or earned money for use in a specific way. For instance, when money is given to a church, it must be used according to the designated purpose and according to proper authority. The financial managers are not owners but stewards of that money. They must ensure that the money is used properly, and anyone who would receive the money must follow the proper procedure and receive the proper authorization.

Fraud. In addition to simple theft, there are other dishonest ways of taking money or property. The Bible teaches us not to defraud other people. (See Leviticus 19:13; Mark 10:19; I Corinthians 6:8; I Thessalonians 4:6.) To defraud means to cheat, swindle, take by trickery, or take by deception. Again, we will give some practical examples to illustrate the concept.

- *Merchants* can defraud by having incorrect weighing scales, by deliberately shortchanging a customer, or by deliberately measuring out less than what a customer actually pays for. They can also defraud by giving damaged goods to an unknowing customer.
- *Sellers* can defraud by giving exaggerated descriptions and creating false impressions. Sellers should answer buyers' questions honestly and should not actively conceal important facts about the items being sold. Salespersons need to make sure that they can honestly recommend the items that they are selling.
- *False pretenses*. It is fraudulent to receive money for one purpose but spend it for something else. For instance, when employees requisition money

to purchase an item, they should spend the money on that item. If they purchase something cheaper and pocket the difference, they have committed fraud. They should refund the difference or obtain permission for alternate use. If a church receives donations for a certain purpose, it must use the money for that purpose or else obtain consent of the donor for a new purpose.

- *False receipts.* It is fraudulent to submit a receipt or expense statement for reimbursement when the actual expenditure is less.
- *False documents.* Forging documents and using false documents is dishonest. It defrauds the person or organization who seeks verification by proper documentation. Likewise, if an employee knowingly accepts false documents, he or she is defrauding the organization that has asked for proper documentation.
- *Omission of important information.* We can be guilty of fraud if we omit valuable and pertinent information when asked to explain something. Withholding truth or telling only a part of the truth can be misleading, and if another person or organization is relying on this inaccurate impression in making a decision, the result can be fraud.
- *Wages and salary.* When people work for wages or salary, they sell their time in exchange for money. Therefore, both parties must honor this mutual agreement. Employers should treat employees fairly, provide reasonable protections and accommodations for them to perform their work, supply the promised benefits, and pay everything

> owed. Employees should work diligently and give an honest day's work, whether the boss is present or not.

Work ethic. In discussing the importance of working diligently, we recognize that employees need time to relax and take breaks, simply to be more effective. There are also times when work is slow. As long as they follow the employer's guidelines and fulfill the work they are assigned to do, they may be able to take some personal time or attend to some personal matters. However, they should not neglect their work or cheat their employer of the time for which they are paid.

Christians should be known for their diligent and faithful work. They should not work merely to please their superiors or create a favorable impression, but they should perform their work as unto the Lord. (See Ephesians 6:5-8.) As representatives of Jesus Christ, their lives are a witness of the gospel. In applying these teachings, Christians should endeavor to come to work on time, depart on time, make up for personal time if necessary, and obtain permission to take time off.

Ministers likewise have a responsibility to work diligently. Pastors who receive income from tithes have a responsibility to minister to people and to work faithfully for the Lord. They should be diligent in contacting the sick, absentees, visitors, and prospects. Since they typically do not have anyone to set a schedule for them, they should discipline themselves to put in a full day's work and to be available when people need them.

Pastors expect the average church member to work a full-time job, attend church services, have personal devotions, and do volunteer work for the church. Therefore, pastors should at least do the same. If their congregational responsibilities do not require all their time, they should invest extra time in personal evangelism and growing a church. If their area of labor is small, they should reach out to other areas. There is always an opportunity to spread the gospel, and there is always more work to do. For self-evaluation, full-time ministers should ask themselves, Apart from personal devotion and time spent in church services, do I spend at least forty hours a week actively working for the kingdom of God?

Paying taxes. Jesus taught us to pay our lawful taxes to the government (Matthew 17:24-27; 22:15-22). Paul wrote, "Render therefore to all their due: taxes to whom taxes are due, customs to whom customs, fear to whom fear, honor to whom honor" (Romans 13:7, NKJV).

If we refuse to pay the taxes we owe, then we are defrauding the government and our fellow citizens. We benefit from the social services that they pay for, yet we do not contribute our fair share. If we are not honest in reporting our income, then we are guilty of lying. If our dishonesty is discovered, then we are subject to civil and criminal penalties, and we bring reproach upon the church.

Paying debts. Christians should avoid unnecessary debt, remembering that "the borrower is servant to the lender" (Proverbs 22:7). It is advisable to save money to purchase consumer items (rather than borrowing money for these things) and to pay credit card bills in full each month. In general, it is wise to incur long-term debt only for items that retain or appreciate in value, such as a home.

If Christians do incur debt, they should discharge

all their obligations in a timely manner. "Owe no man anything, but to love one another" (Romans 13:8). "Let no debt remain outstanding, except the continuing debt to love one another" (NIV). If we borrow money with a promise to pay it back by a certain date, then we should keep our commitment. When we purchase something by a credit card or an installment plan, we do not owe the money until the agreed-upon due date. If we do not pay on time, then we are in violation of God's Word.

If we borrow, we must repay and repay on time. If we borrow something without returning it, we have committed theft. If we borrow money without the intention to repay, or without a reasonable expectation that we can repay it, we have also committed fraud.

Due to an unforeseen problem, sometimes we may not be able to pay a debt on time. In that case, we need to follow the procedure allowed by the creditor to pay at a later date with a late fee. If there is no such arrangement, then we must contact our creditor, provide an explanation, and ask for an extension of time. If we do not repay, we have violated Romans 13:8, unless the creditor releases us.

In cases of extreme hardship, the law allows for the discharge of debts through bankruptcy, but discharging debts legally is not necessarily the same as discharging debts morally. The debtor should carefully consider what action is necessary to be honest in the sight of God. For example, understandable reasons for bankruptcy might be a business failure, medical crisis, loss of job, or other unexpected circumstance that was contrary to the debtor's intention and beyond the debtor's control. The debtor may conclude that a moral way to discharge debts would be to turn over business assets to creditors, cooperate with the repossession of a vehicle, or cooperate with the foreclosure of a home.

Consumer debt is a different matter, however. What if the bankruptcy was caused by extravagant spending or poor money management, and what if the debtor has already enjoyed the benefits of the expenditures—such as restaurant meals, clothing, trips, furnishings, and electronic items? In this case, there is a moral obligation to pay for what the debtor used.

Occasionally a problem arises when someone starts a project "by faith." One pastor did not have the funds to build a church, but he ordered the materials "by faith" and began to build. Later he could not pay his debts. The result was that the minister and the church obtained a bad name in the community. He did not operate by faith but by foolishness.

If a church wants to build, they should put their faith to work by raising and saving funds, obtaining proper credit with a reasonable and affordable plan of repayment, and building as they have the means. They should do what they can and wait for the next development by faith. They can have faith for God to supply the necessary money before they spend it. Jesus said, "For which of you, intending to build a tower, sitteth not down first, and counteth the cost, whether he have sufficient to finish it?" (Luke 14:28).

Problems can arise when someone borrows from another person in the church. One deacon borrowed money from an individual, saying the church needed it. Actually he needed it personally and had no means of repaying the debt. Because he lied, he owed money that he could not repay, and he caused others to lose confidence in the church.

Making and guaranteeing loans. On a personal level, when people are truly in need and we have the means to help them, we should act generously. Jesus said, "Give to him that asketh thee, and from him that would borrow of thee turn not thou away" (Matthew 5:42). This statement appears in the context of Christ's teaching on loving one another and being reconciled to one another. Thus, it assumes some sort of personal relationship rather than a business transaction. Those making such a request have an honest need that is known to the prospective donors, and the donors can easily meet the need from their personal resources without impairing their ability to meet their own obligations.

When people are persistently in need, however, or when their circumstances are not known to the potential donors, a loan or gift may not be the best way to help them. Instead, they may need help to find employment, overcome destructive personal habits, or develop a budget to live within their means. In this case, it is probably best to refer them to the church or a social agency that can ascertain their needs and establish a means of accountability. Individual donors can make wise use of their money by giving to these programs.

Sometimes people ask others to serve as guarantors or co-signers on a personal loan. Such a request should serve as a warning, for it indicates that the borrower may not have the means to repay the loan. There is a high risk of default, in which case the guarantor will be liable. "He who is surety for a stranger will suffer, but one who hates being surety is secure" (Proverbs 11:15, NKJV). "A man devoid of understanding shakes hands in a pledge, and becomes surety for his friend" (Proverbs 17:18, NKJV). Consequently, the best policy is not to guarantee a personal loan unless the guarantor is willing and able to assume the primary responsibility for the loan if necessary.

Extortion. Extortioners will not inherit the kingdom of God (I Corinthians 6:10). In fact, Christians are commanded not to have fellowship with those who call themselves believers but who are extortioners (I Corinthians 5:11). To extort means to obtain money or favors by violence, threat, or misuse of authority. One form of extortion is blackmail—using a threat of exposure. Here are some examples of extortion.

- Mr. A stole money before he became a Christian. An old acquaintance, Mr. B, demanded that A help him get a job at A's office. If not, then B threatened to reveal A's past life with the result that A would probably be fired. B is guilty of extortion, even though a favor is involved and not money.
- Mr. A always left the office when the manager was gone. Once Miss B asked A to give her some office postage stamps under A's control. When A refused, B threatened to tell the manager about A's absence. A is guilty of fraud, but B is guilty of extortion.
- A preacher lived in a house owned by the church. Because of problems the church asked him to resign, but he refused to leave the parsonage unless the church gave him a large sum of money. Of course, his continuing presence would have caused severe problems for the church. Although the preacher did not use physical force, he used a

threat of harm.

Usury and interest. Several passages in the Old Testament warn against usury (Psalm 15:5). In its original, general sense, the word refers to interest on loans. The Israelites were not to charge interest on loans to the poor or on loans for food (Exodus 22:25; Leviticus 25:36-37). In general, they were not to charge interest on loans to fellow Israelites but only to foreigners (Deuteronomy 23:19-20). These statements occur in the context of personal loans in an agrarian society as a means of helping one another, not in a business context.

These instructions indicate that the charging of interest is not wrong under all circumstances. Rather, the concern was not to profit unjustly or excessively, especially when dealing with basic necessities of personal life. Later warnings against usury focus on this sense of justice, speaking of both "usury" and "increase" (Proverbs 28:8; Ezekiel 18:8-17). The NIV uses "exorbitant interest" in the former passage and "usury" and "excessive interest" in the latter. Indeed, in modern usage, the word *usury* means exorbitant, unconscionable, or excessive interest, such as interest charged by a loan shark.

The New Testament does not have any specific teaching on the subject. Jesus told two parables about lazy servants, whom He rebuked for not earning interest with the money that their masters had entrusted to them (Matthew 25:27; Luke 19:23). In a commercial sense, interest is the cost of using money, representing the real cost of forgoing other uses of the money. In a business context, the Lord recognized that it was legitimate to pay and collect interest.

Bribes and gifts. The Bible teaches against bribery.

A bribe is "something, such as money or a favor, offered or given to a person in a position of trust to influence that person's views or conduct."[1] Giving a gift is wrong when the intention is to gain an unfair advantage or an unlawful favor in return.

Gifts can blind the wise and cause the righteous to sin. "And thou shalt take no gift: for the gift blindeth the wise, and perverteth the words of the righteous" (Exodus 23:8). Deuteronomy 16:18-19 repeats the same words and adds, "Judges and officers . . . shall judge the people with just judgment. Thou shalt not wrest judgment; thou shalt not respect persons, neither take a gift." A wicked person takes a gift to pervert the course of justice (Proverbs 17:23), and the hands of evildoers are filled with bribes (Psalm 26:10). "A gift destroyeth the heart" (Ecclesiastes 7:7).

Of course, there are times to give and receive gifts, but we must be careful in doing so. Any gift that obligates someone could become an occasion for sin. If a gift distorts fair judgment or results in an illicit favor, then the giver and recipient are guilty of the sin of bribery. Moreover, if someone demands a gift, either directly or indirectly, for the simple performance of a duty, then he or she is guilty of extortion. The sons of Samuel sinned by accepting bribes (I Samuel 8:3).

Isaiah 33:15-16 describes the type of person who pleases God: "He that walketh righteously, and speaketh uprightly; he that despiseth the gain of oppressions, that shaketh his hands from holding of bribes, . . . He shall dwell on high." Such people despise deceit and unjust gain. They do not extort, oppress the poor, take advantage of people, or deal falsely. They do not seek or expect bribes and refuse to accept them if offered.

Ministers should not accept money in return for helping individuals spiritually, such as praying for someone or baptizing someone. The reason is that the gospel and its benefits are free. "Heal the sick, cleanse the lepers, raise the dead, cast out devils: freely ye have received, freely give" (Matthew 10:8).

Peter rebuked Simon for trying to purchase the ability to bestow the Holy Spirit (Acts 8:19-20). The prophet Elisha refused to accept a gift from Naaman when the latter was healed of leprosy. When Gehazi, Elisha's servant, secretly accepted gifts from Naaman anyway, he was stricken with leprosy. Elisha rebuked him: "Is it a time to receive money, and to receive garments?" (II Kings 5:26-27). If people who receive blessings from God want to give an offering of thanks, they can give it to the church.

Sometimes leaders receive gifts because someone wants to obligate them. After the gift is accepted, the giver asks for an inappropriate or impermissible favor. Therefore, leaders should use wisdom in accepting gifts. Depending on the circumstances, they may refuse a gift, return it, or at least take care that it does not influence them improperly. Here are some examples:

- A man is in charge of hiring workers for his company. Someone he does not know gives him a present. He may thereby feel obligated to hire that person, but he cannot let the gift influence him. If he does, then he is not being fair to other applicants. He may pass up a more qualified candidate and thereby cheat his company. In this case, it is best to refuse the gift.
- A woman in the church does something wrong

and hurts many people. Biblically, she needs to seek reconciliation and forgiveness, but instead she brings a cake to the pastor. The pastor cannot allow this gift to override biblical requirements and solutions.

- A new employee is eager to make friends and be accepted within the company. A fellow employee asks him to do an illegitimate favor, such as accepting a false document. If he complies, he will earn goodwill, which could result in a return favor or greater job security. Although there is no explicit offer of a gift, this action is still dishonest and a form of bribery.

In many parts of the world, corruption is rampant. Often it is impossible to conduct legitimate business with certain officials unless they receive a gift. They refuse to grant a necessary approval unless they receive extra money. Can Christians conscientiously give them a gift in this case?

On the part of the officials, this behavior is a form of extortion and solicitation of bribery. As a society we should try to eliminate such practices. If Christians give a gift in order to seek a preference over others or for an official to overlook something wrong on their part, then they are guilty of bribery. However, if they are forced to offer a gift so that an official will treat them fairly, or so that an official will do his or her job, then they have not done wrong. They are not asking for anything illegal or unethical but simply for proper and just treatment.

In short, the Bible instructs us not to accept bribes. We can accept gifts only if they do not obligate us. We must not let any gift or favor taint our conscience or pervert our judgment. In turn, we should not try to obligate anyone else to act inappropriately through gifts or favors.

Honesty and integrity today. As in the days before the Flood, it seems as if the whole earth is corrupt (Genesis 6:11). Corruption has been uncovered in high levels of government, politics, business, and even religion. There are many religious charlatans and extortioners. Businesspersons, government employees, lawyers, accountants, leaders of all kinds, and even ordinary workers are exposed to frequent temptations to compromise their honesty and integrity.

In this environment, we must cherish and protect our integrity, because in the end it is all we have. Once lost, it is difficult to regain. Blessed are those who keep their word even when it hurts them to do so (Psalm 15:4-5)! Blessed are those who will not sell their integrity at any price! "For what is a man profited, if he shall gain the whole world, and lose his own soul? or what shall a man give in exchange for his soul?" (Matthew 16:26).

Note

[1]*The American Heritage Dictionary of the English Language*, 3d ed.

CHAPTER

12

Authority and Organization in the Church

And God hath set some in the church . . . governments (I Corinthians 12:28).

Holiness is connected to church government. Specifically, what authority, if any, does the church have with regard to the implementation of holiness? Does the church have authority or responsibility to discipline those who do not follow its teachings? What does holiness teach about relationships among saints?

Authority in the church. The church is the body of called-out believers who have been born again and who are endeavoring to live holy lives. It is not synonymous with any human organization, nor is it limited to such. Membership in a particular denomination is not a prerequisite of salvation. At the same time, God has blessed human organizations, and they have done much to advance the gospel.

The church is founded upon the Word of God, and all authority in the church is subject to the Word of God. Each person is responsible to believe and obey God's Word, and each person is responsible for his or her own salvation. We cannot follow leaders into false doctrine, sin, or unethical practices.

God has instituted authority and organization in His church. He has ordained relationships among believers, and He has established a framework for fellowship.

From the beginning, the church has had some structure. Jesus personally chose and trained twelve apostles to be leaders of the church, and He appointed Judas to be the first treasurer of the group (John 13:29).

God has placed governments (administrations) in the church (I Corinthians 12:28). He has given the fivefold ministry to the church (Ephesians 4:11). He has also endowed people in the church with gifts of prophesying, ministering, teaching, exhorting, and ruling or leading (Romans 12:4-8).

Organization in the early church. The Book of Acts records a history of organized effort, recognition of leadership, unified decision-making, and mutual fellowship.

In Acts 1:15-26, the 120 founding members of the apostolic church met to choose a successor to Judas. Peter apparently chaired the meeting. The group established qualifications for the office of apostle, nominated two men, and ultimately chose Matthias by lot.

After the outpouring of the Holy Spirit, the people "continued stedfastly in the apostles' doctrine and fellowship" (Acts 2:42). They acknowledged the leadership of the Twelve—including Matthias, whom they had chosen—in doctrinal teaching and in maintaining fellowship.

They also acknowledged the apostles' leadership in the collection and distribution of church funds (Acts 4:35).

In Acts 6, the Twelve once again called a meeting of all believers to institute a system for taking care of church business matters. The assembly chose seven men to administer business affairs under the leadership of the apostles, so that the latter could devote more time to prayer and preaching. The apostles first stipulated that the men be full of the Holy Ghost and wisdom. Then the assembly chose the seven, and the apostles prayed and laid hands on them. Laying on of hands is one of the basic doctrines of the church (Hebrews 6:2), and it is administered so that God will bless, heal, or anoint someone for a special purpose. In this instance, it showed that God, through the leaders, had authorized and approved of the election of these men.

Philip, one of the seven, later brought the gospel to Samaria. When revival broke out there, the apostles sent Peter and John to investigate, oversee, and help. Under their leadership, the Samaritans received the Holy Spirit (Acts 8:14-17).

In Acts 11, the apostles and brethren of Judea asked the apostle Peter to report to them. He had just preached to Cornelius, a Gentile, and the leaders wanted to find out if his actions were valid or not. Even though Peter had been the most noticeable leader up to this point, had received the keys of the kingdom from Jesus, and had received direct orders from the Lord to preach to Cornelius, he still submitted to the authority of the church. He was examined, criticized by some in the meeting, and answered those in authority.

The Jerusalem church sent Barnabas to Antioch to

investigate the growth of the church there, which they had not founded (Acts 11:22-30). His mission was to provide teaching and leadership. Barnabas stayed in Antioch, later bringing in Paul as his assistant. Prophets also came from Jerusalem to help. Soon afterwards, the Antioch church took up a collection for the needy in the Jerusalem church and sent the offering to the Jerusalem elders by Barnabas and Paul.

The Antioch church grew and developed prophets and teachers of its own. God called Barnabas and Paul to missionary work, revealing this call not only to them but also to the leadership in Antioch. The Antioch ministry then prayed for them, laid hands on them, and appointed them as missionaries (Acts 13:1-4). They went out, establishing churches and ordaining ministers to take charge of them (Acts 14:23).

Acts 15 records the next significant meeting of the church. By this time, the church had grown tremendously. It was no longer just a local congregation in Jerusalem, but it had spread all across Judea, Samaria, and the Gentile nations. In what we could call the first general conference of the church, leaders and ministers from various local congregations gathered in Jerusalem to discuss a hotly debated issue. The question was whether Gentile Christians had to be circumcised and had to keep the law of Moses. There was much discussion and disputing, with Paul, Barnabas, and Peter taking the position that the Gentiles did not have to follow these rituals. Certain believing Pharisees took the opposite point of view. James, the brother of the Lord, chaired the meeting and announced the decision that the majority supported.

After the decision was made, the church united behind the result and chose representatives to communicate it to local churches. The church exercised its authority to decide what was binding on Gentile believers. (See Matthew 18:18.) Specifically, they decided that Gentiles were required to obey four teachings from the law of Moses, because "it seemed good to the Holy Ghost, and to us" (Acts 15:28-29).

After this meeting, Paul becomes the major figure in the Book of Acts. Although his position had been vindicated, Paul came to Jerusalem after his third missionary journey to give a report to James and the other leaders in Jerusalem. They rejoiced to hear his report but then advised him to take certain Jewish vows in order to appease the Jewish Christian community. He followed their advice in order to foster unity and in submission to their authority (Acts 21:18-26).

The Epistles provide further evidence of a healthy, close-knit organization for the purposes of mutual fellowship, establishing ministerial standards, and collecting offerings. James, Peter, and John were pillars, or general leaders, of the church (Galatians 2:9). This fact did not prevent Paul from rebuking Peter and others when they did wrong (Galatians 2:11-14). Under Jewish pressure, Peter had withdrawn from fellowship with Gentiles. Consequently, he "walked not uprightly according to the truth of the gospel."

Paul was the overseer of a number of churches that he had founded on his missionary journeys and to which he wrote letters of instruction, encouragement, and warning. He appointed overseers and ministers to work under him. Timothy became the overseer in Ephesus (I Timothy 1:3).

Titus was the overseer of Crete and had responsibility for ordaining ministers in that area (Titus 1:5).

To aid these two ministers in organizing their respective areas, Paul gave them a list of qualifications for ministerial leaders (I Timothy 3:1-7; Titus 1:5-16). These passages use the terms *bishop* (meaning "overseer") and *elder* interchangeably for the pastors of local churches. Paul also gave qualifications for deacons, leaders who assist pastors in church affairs (I Timothy 3:8-13). Paul wrote a letter of recommendation for Titus and another brother, sending them to various churches to receive offerings for the Jerusalem church (II Corinthians 8:16-24). He promoted a plan of receiving offerings every Sunday, and he asked the Corinthian church to recommend someone to bring an offering to Jerusalem (I Corinthians 16:1-3).

The apostle John sent a letter of recommendation for a minister named Demetrius along with a warning not to accept Diotrephes (III John 9-12). Jesus and Paul outlined procedures for settling disputes in the church, for judging sinners in the church, and for withdrawing fellowship from members if necessary (Matthew 18:15-18; I Corinthians 5:1-13). Paul warned the elders in Ephesus about false prophets (Acts 20:28-30), and the Lord commended that church for discerning and testing false apostles (Revelation 2:2).

These passages of Scripture show that there was close cooperation among the churches, ways of handling problems, and lines of authority. At the local level we find elders (pastors) in charge of the local churches, assisted by deacons. Then there were overseers in charge of regions or groups of churches, such as Titus in Crete. In turn, Paul supervised Titus as well as some churches Paul had founded. His special ministry was directing the missionary outreach to the Gentiles, even as Peter directed the outreach to the Jews (Galatians 2:7-8). Peter was a major spokesman and representative of the early church, while James was apparently the chief leader in Jerusalem.

Thus, each church and each minister operated under the authority of leaders. Even the highest leaders such as Peter and Paul exhorted each other and were subject to the church as a whole. Both of them gave reports to and received advice from the assembly of ministers that gathered in Jerusalem. These examples show that church government supersedes personal positions, even ministries ordained by God.

The authority of leadership. The Bible teaches us to follow godly leadership. "Remember them which have the rule over you, who have spoken unto you the word of God: whose faith follow, considering the end of their conversation [conduct]. . . . Obey them that have the rule over you, and submit yourselves: for they watch for your souls, as they that must give account, that they may do it with joy, and not with grief: for that is unprofitable for you" (Hebrews 13:7, 17). "And we beseech you, brethren, to know them which labour among you, and are over you in the Lord, and admonish you; and to esteem them very highly in love for their work's sake" (I Thessalonians 5:12-13).

These principles apply to all Christians at every level, to leadership among churches as well as leadership within local churches. According to these verses, we are to discern the character of leaders, follow their genuine faith, and esteem them highly for their labor. While we recognize that all humans are fallible, we respect the offices that God has given them. We esteem people in authority because God has given them authority to do their jobs. "Let every soul be subject unto the higher powers. For there is no power but of God: the powers that be are ordained of God" (Romans 13:1). (See also verses 2-7.) This principle applies to society and also to the church. "Let the elders that rule well be counted worthy of double honour, especially they who labour in the word and doctrine" (I Timothy 5:17).

The purpose of leadership in the church is "for the perfecting of the saints, for the work of the ministry, for the edifying of the body of Christ" (Ephesians 4:11-12). The job of a minister is to "reprove, rebuke, exhort with all longsuffering and doctrine" (II Timothy 4:2).

People who do not heed the voice of authority are on dangerous ground, even if they are ministers or leaders themselves. Jude 8 warns about those who "despise dominion, and speak evil of dignities." Peter also taught against those who "despise government. Presumptuous are they, self-willed, they are not afraid to speak evil of dignities." They shall "utterly perish in their own corruption; and shall receive the reward of unrighteousness" (II Peter 2:10-13). One of the signs of the end time is an erosion of God-given authority in the home, in society, and in the church (II Timothy 3:2, 8).

In the New Testament, government was present in the local church and also extended beyond it. The general church body sent leaders to inquire about local congregations, sent missionaries to establish new churches, sent ministers to teach local congregations, resolved doctrinal disputes, organized collections of money, sent letters of recommendation for evangelists, withdrew fellowship from church members who persisted in open sin, warned local churches concerning false prophets, and judged false prophets among them.

The general church body has authority to make a decision on new issues that may confront it from time to time. By means of a general conference, the early church established guidelines for the conduct of Gentile believers, based on scriptural precedent and the principles of the gospel (Acts 15). The early church also set forth qualifications for apostles, missionaries, ministers, and deacons, and it chose eligible people to fill these offices. Jesus did not explicitly address many of these issues in His earthly ministry, but He gave authority to the church to handle these matters. No individual took it upon himself or herself to make and promulgate these decisions, but the general church did.

In our day, the church faces various circumstances that were unknown in New Testament times. It has some authority and responsibility to respond to these new conditions, applying scriptural principles to modern situations. At the same time, we recognize that only Scripture is our infallible authority; all human decisions are potentially fallible and subject to correction or change.

Judgment in the church. In general, individual Christians are not to judge others, meaning that we cannot judge their heart, motives, or standing with God (Matthew 7:1; Romans 14:10; James 4:12). At the same time, as a practical matter we can identify inappropriate conduct and adjust our conduct accordingly. We can recognize the fruit that people bear and make a personal decision not to partake of evil fruit (Luke 6:44). We also have a responsibility to judge prophecy and to test the spirits to see if they are of God (I Corinthians 14:29; I John 4:1).

The church leadership has authority to make judgments for the good of the body and to deal with open, unrepented sin in its midst. In addition, the church has authority to make judgments in disputes between saints.

Jesus gave the following procedure in case of a conflict between two believers (Matthew 18:15-18):

1. The aggrieved party should go to the other person privately in an attempt to resolve the matter. If we know that another believer has something against us, we should first go to that person and be reconciled. Then we can come to the altar to offer our gifts to God (Matthew 5:23-24).
2. If the attempt at resolution does not work, then the aggrieved person should take two or three witnesses with him in a second attempt to resolve the problem. The church may designate mature believers who are capable of mediation in such situations.
3. If the problem is not resolved, then it should be brought to the church. At this point, it should be handled by those in leadership, who can establish a method of judging the matter. For instance, perhaps the pastors (elders) and church board (deacons) would need to decide on a matter.
4. If someone refuses to heed the judgment of the church, then he or she is to be removed from fellowship and considered to be an unbeliever. If the church and its leadership have been fair and honest in their decision, God will honor it.

Lawsuits. Believers should use the foregoing procedure to handle disputes in the church. They should not sue one another in civil court (I Corinthians 6:1-8). The reason is that saints are training to be judges of angels and of the millennial kingdom. If we cannot settle our own disputes now, how can we judge angels and the world later? Moreover, a lawsuit between saints sets a bad example in front of unbelievers. It is better to be defrauded than to present a picture of church strife before the eyes of the world.

It may be appropriate to sue someone who is not in the church or who does not submit to the authority of the church, for the above reasons would not apply. For example, it may be necessary to go to court to defend freedom of religion or to recover damages due to an automobile accident. At the same time, we should keep in mind Christ's teaching to be generous, not to seek revenge, and to love our enemies. In this context, Jesus taught that we should do more than what is legally required, and if we are found to be at fault in a court of law then we should be willing to compensate more than the minimum. (See Matthew 5:38-42.)

What should we do if one saint wrongs another or even the whole church but refuses to follow the judgment of the church? After the above procedure has been followed, eventually he or she will be removed from the church, and in some cases it may be appropriate to turn to the civil courts for a remedy.

As an example, let us suppose a church officer falsely places church property in his own name. Two or three representatives of the church should confront him and ask him to correct his wrong. If he refuses, the church should judge the matter. In this case it would be appropriate for the elders and deacons, or the church board, to review the evidence. If they find that he has done wrong, and if he still refuses to comply, he should be removed from fellowship. The purpose is to impress upon him the seriousness of his sin; to cleanse the church of ongoing, unrepented sin; and to dissociate him from the church in the eyes of the world. After this action, the church can pursue the matter in civil court.

Church discipline. As we have seen, one reason to remove a person from fellowship is because of a refusal to submit to church judgment. In I Corinthians 5:1-13, Paul gave additional grounds. (See chapter 13 for further definition.)

The problem in Corinth was that a man in the church was committing incest. The church was proud of its spiritual gifts, yet it had overlooked this sin. Paul rebuked them for not judging the sin and removing the offender from fellowship.

When people who are recognized as church members live in open, notorious, unrepented sin, they present a false message to the world about what the church stands for. They discourage believers who are trying to live a holy life, and they deceive themselves and others into thinking that they are acceptable in God's sight.

The proper course of action in such cases is to remove the offenders from fellowship—delivering them to the world, to the kingdom of Satan. The purpose is not punitive but redemptive. By this action, the offenders may be jarred into repentance. They may suffer at the hands of Satan to such an extent that they will repent and return to the church. There is yet hope that they can be saved through appropriate church discipline. As long as the church ignores or covers up their sin, however, they are unlikely to see the need for repentance.

This type of judgment extends to those who call themselves believers but who are fornicators, covetous, idolaters, railers (revilers), drunkards, or extortioners. When people are removed from fellowship for one of these reasons, believers are not to have fellowship with them, not even to eat with them. Believers should still love them, care for them, and offer them assistance as needed, but they cannot treat them as members of the church. The reason is that the offenders need to realize the reality of their backslidden condition.

Sometimes people in the church continue to have close fellowship with those who have been excommunicated for notorious, ongoing sins. If we do this, however, we support their rebellion, diminish their chances of repenting, confuse faithful saints, and confuse onlookers. Moreover, we engage in fellowship with the rebellious and unclean spirit of those people—a spirit that can affect us in the same way.

Once, a minister was removed from fellowship for getting drunk in the town where he pastored and for immoral advances to a number of girls. Within a few months, he went to another area and began to preach and hold revivals. He showed no signs of repentance. Some who knew him went to help him, saying, "Well, he is still a preacher." Contrary to this example, however, we cannot support the ministry of someone who has lost the biblical qualifications for being a preacher.

Those who acknowledge their sin, or those who do not profess to remain church members, can be treated with a greater degree of openness and friendship. The reason is that our friendship with them does not send a wrong message to them, to believers, or to the world. Everyone understands their status, and it brings no reproach upon the church.

When people have done wrong but repent, there is no need to remove them from fellowship. They may have lost their qualifications for a leadership position, in which case they should not continue to function in that role until they regain their qualifications. Sometimes, they need time to refocus, reconsecrate, and reestablish spiritual disciplines. This process is sometimes called silencing.

This type of discipline is necessary when leaders have lost a good reputation or when they need to prove themselves for a time. Otherwise, even though they have repented, they may bring reproach on the church or create a stumbling block for others who have lost confidence in them. If the wrongdoers are truly repentant, they will cooperate with reasonable restrictions of this nature and will not try to evade discipline by going to another church or organization. "Now no chastening for the present seemeth to be joyous, but grievous: nevertheless afterward it yieldeth the peaceable fruit of righteousness unto them which are exercised thereby" (Hebrews 12:11). The disciplinary process usually reveals whether the wrongdoers have repented and whether they have the humility to prove themselves faithful. If they are patient, they will be rewarded.

It is advisable to handle these situations as quietly, discreetly, and kindly as the circumstances will allow. In many cases, those who have done wrong can voluntarily step away from their responsibilities for a time of refreshing and refocusing. If they truly recognize the value of the discipline, they can simply explain to leaders and friends that they are stepping down for personal reasons but plan to become involved once again after a sabbatical. Since there can be various reasons why people need to take time off, there should be no undue speculation or concern, especially if they continue to be faithful to church.

If ministers commit a sin that does not permanently disqualify them from their ministry, they can be silenced or put on probation by those in authority. After a certain time, they can be reinstated fully if they have been faithful during the probation.

Such discipline does not mean that humans are taking away the calling of God. God is the one who has established government in the church as well as qualifications for ministry. Those in authority have the responsibility to administer God's plan, and we should not despise them for it. Many times leaders are wounded by criticism from a wrongdoer that they had to discipline and from friends of the wrongdoer. Usually, because of the need for confidentiality, they cannot fully explain the reasons for their decision but must stand on principle. Many times leaders must discipline those they love and those who are personal friends. They cannot condone or tolerate sin, but they must apply the Word of God without favoritism, and they must act for the good of the whole church.

Sometimes, ministers permanently disqualify themselves by notorious sins such as adultery or criminal activity. If they repent, they can be accepted into the assembly and can find a place to work in the local assembly. Instead of evading spiritual discipline, they need to find suitable capacities in which they can serve as faithful and valuable workers, and we should assist them in this process.

Let us not be self-willed and disobedient. If we do wrong, let us find a place of repentance and accept discipline from godly leaders. Let us prove ourselves faithful to the Lord, His church, and His Word, and work even harder for His kingdom.

Public rebuke. The best way to deal with problems is by preventive maintenance, by teaching the principles of Christian living and holiness to the congregation. When problems arise, it is generally best to handle them on an individual basis, as privately and discreetly as possible. Galatians 6:1 says, "If a man be overtaken in a fault, ye which are spiritual, restore such an one in the spirit of meekness; considering thyself, lest thou also be tempted."

It is almost never beneficial for a pastor to publicly rebuke someone by name or identifying description. There are rare occasions, however, when a situation must be addressed publicly for the good of the body. For example, when someone must be removed from fellowship for notorious sin, it may be necessary to announce this fact. Due to privacy concerns, however, it is best not to make a specific allegation but to make a general statement and then only in a closed meeting restricted to those who have a legal right and need to know, such as leaders or possibly voting members of the assembly. Public rebuke may be justified when a person attempts to destroy the church through open rebellion and sowing of discord. In general, we should not resort to this measure unless we have prayerfully considered the matter and feel constrained by the Holy Spirit.

If someone sins but repents, usually no public confession or rebuke is necessary. In general, confession should be as public as the sin. If the sin has seriously affected the entire body, then a public apology or public acknowledgment of the situation may be advisable as a form of discipline, correction, or resolution of the matter. Again, to protect privacy concerns and the dignity of all concerned, it is best for a public statement to be general and to focus on repentance and reconciliation.

A situation that requires some form of public notice or rebuke is when a ministerial leader persists in open sin. Speaking of elders, Paul instructed, "Them that sin rebuke before all, that others also may fear" (I Timothy 5:20). The Greek present tense here indicates ongoing sin.

It is not appropriate for leaders to act out of rage, bitterness, malice, or resentment. Preachers should not lash out against people from the pulpit in anger over a situation, "for the wrath of man worketh not the righteousness of God" (James 1:20).

Reproof and rebuke are part of the ministry of the Word (II Timothy 4:2). The Spirit of God will reprove the world of sin (John 16:8). The word *reprove* means to test, put on trial, examine, convict, refute, expose, bring to shame. Sometimes, this work takes place privately and sometimes publicly.

Occasionally, a worship leader or pastor will need to rebuke someone who is causing confusion in a church service. Often the problem can be handled diplomatically by changing the order of the service, but sometimes the leader must give private or even public instructions. As shepherds of the flock, pastors have the responsibility to ensure that everything is done decently and in order

(I Corinthians 14:33, 40). Public worship needs to be in spirit and in truth—in accordance with the moving of the Spirit and in accordance with the Bible. For example, there should be no more than three messages in tongues and interpretation or prophecy in one service, and the leader should see that this teaching is followed (I Corinthians 14:27-29).

"Touch not mine anointed, and do my prophets no harm" (I Chronicles 16:22). In the context, the "anointed" are the Israelites, the collective people of God. The verse tells us that God will protect His people and will punish those who attack them. It also teaches that God will support and defend His leaders. It does not give leaders authority to abuse people, establish a dictatorship, or exempt themselves from spiritual authority in their own lives.

The Bible teaches respect for those in positions of authority. God often uses someone in authority to accomplish His plan even if that person does not always do His will. He appointed a pagan king, Cyrus, to fulfill His purpose (Isaiah 44:28-45:3), and He spoke to His people through another pagan king, Necho (II Chronicles 35:20-24). God sent a spirit of prophecy upon backslidden King Saul (I Samuel 19:23-24). He gave a word of prophecy through the hypocritical high priest Caiaphas specifically because of his office. Caiaphas actually was plotting to kill Jesus and did not realize the meaning of his own words, but God spoke through him in spite of him (John 11:49-52). If God could use these sinful men because of their positions, how much more can He use sincere, honest, godly leaders even when we think they are mistaken?

The Bible also indicates that we should not take individual action to oppose a leader before God has removed that leader from office. It is unscriptural to act rebelliously against a God-called leader or to stir up discord and strife. God enforced the authority of Moses against the complaints of his older brother and sister, Aaron and Miriam, and against the rebellion of Korah.

Even when leaders are wrong, we need to treat them with respect, pray for God's direction, and wait for God to work out the situation. King Saul had backslidden and Samuel had anointed David to become the next king, but even then David refused to act against Saul. Out of jealousy, Saul hunted David and tried to kill him. On two occasions during this time, David had the opportunity to kill Saul, but he did not, even though he would have seemingly accomplished God's will. As long as Saul was king, David respected his position and anointing.

Leaders need to realize that they are subject to authority themselves. In I Kings 2:13-27, God chose Solomon to succeed David as king. Solomon's older half brother Adonijah entered into a conspiracy with Abiathar, the priest, and Joab, the general, to become king instead. When the plot was discovered, Solomon executed Adonijah and Joab. He also removed Abiathar from the priesthood but did not kill him because of his past services to God and to David. Solomon had respect for his position as priest but still removed him from office. He had respect but also judgment.

Solomon had the authority to remove Abiathar from the priesthood because Abiathar had lost his qualification by his own rebellious actions. Solomon was God's chosen ruler over the nation, and he had the authority to judge Abiathar.

Some claim that if ministers are disciplined in any way then the church is interfering with God's calling and anointing. As we have seen, however, the church does have authority to make certain judgments. When leaders sin, the church has not taken away their anointing, but they have disqualified themselves by their own actions. Indeed, Paul rebuked the Corinthian church for not judging sin in a certain situation. He asked if there was no one wise enough to judge, and if not, how they would be able to judge the world later. (See I Corinthians 5:1-13; 6:1-5.)

Although God anoints people for ministry and places them into positions, He has given qualifications for the church to implement and authority for the church to exercise. When dealing with problems, we need to seek God's leading and timing, but God has already revealed His will in certain situations. Church members should not rebel against authority, but when there are problems in leadership they can and should inform those who have the authority to deal with that type of situation.

"Touch not mine anointed" does not give any leader or minister immunity from authority and discipline. It did not save Abiathar from being put away from the priesthood when he rebelled. Neither did it prevent Ezra and Nehemiah from removing from the priesthood a large number of men who did not have the proper qualifications (Ezra 2:61-63; Nehemiah 7:63-65).

Errors in leadership. What if a pastor or other leader seems to be in error? If the error relates to a method, program, or plan, we should be humble and submissive. Despite differences of opinion, we need to respect and follow godly leaders. We never have the right to murmur, complain, or sow discord. (See chapters 3 and 4.) If we want to change a situation, we can pray for God to work things out. Sometimes it is appropriate to offer respectful suggestions directly to the leader in question or other designated leaders. God could use our input to help resolve the difficulty. If in good conscience we cannot actively cooperate with a certain plan, then at least we should do nothing to obstruct or undermine it.

If a leader is operating unethically, living in sin, or teaching false doctrine, then we should not follow the leader in this area. Instead, we should bring the matter to the attention of those who have authority to deal with it. No one should follow leadership into spiritual error or positions contrary to the Word of God. We follow leaders as long as they follow Christ. (See I Corinthians 11:1; Galatians 1:8.)

In every institution, there are proper procedures that provide for a change of policy or leadership. It is not wrong to change policy or replace leadership, if it is done with the right attitude and under the proper authority.

Independence. Everyone should submit to God-given government and authority. For this reason, it is dangerous to operate independently. Those who work independently still need to have a system of authority and accountability. They still need to meet biblical qualifications.

Leaders who do not want to work with others need to examine themselves. Often, there is an unwillingness to submit to biblical authority. Some ministers insist that their church members submit to their authority, but they themselves refuse to submit to any kind of church government. They emphasize that people should pay tithes, and some maintain complete personal control over the tithes, but to whom do they pay tithes and to whom are they accountable financially? They exercise strong control over people, but from whom do they accept advice and leadership?

Some people hop from church to church and even from organization to organization. They usually have a problem submitting to leadership. If they rebel against godly leadership, then they rebel against God. Such people need to ask why they cannot be content where God has placed them. Is everyone else wrong, or do they have a problem accepting authority?

Joining a particular denomination is not a requirement of salvation. It is God's will, however, for everyone to associate with a local group of believers—"not forsaking the assembling of ourselves together, as the manner of some is" (Hebrews 10:25). It is also God's will for each local congregation to operate under the authority of a God-called ministry. (See Ephesians 4:11-16; II Timothy 4:1-4; Hebrews 13:7, 17.)

Based on the evidence in Acts and the Epistles, it is God's plan for each local congregation and minister to associate with a larger group of believers. In most cases, it is not advisable to switch churches or work independently. If, after prayerful consideration, a change is needed, it is still important to have fellowship with a group of true believers, to be accountable to the body, and to follow godly leadership.

Every group will eventually have fellowship with someone, and it is important to have fellowship with people of proven character, doctrine, and convictions. (See chapter 13.) God is at work among many different religious groups, but it is dangerous to enter indiscriminately into close fellowship with everyone that God is trying to lead to greater truth. We can be friendly toward them and seek to influence them in a positive direction, but if we have close fellowship with them we could weaken our own beliefs and lifestyle.

Frequently, an independent group finds fellowship with people who do not have strong beliefs or accepts people with unknown or questionable backgrounds. The result can be a conglomeration of people, many of whom are disgruntled, hypocritical, or rebellious. It is difficult for an isolated group to maintain a strong position of holiness and doctrinal purity, but in unity there is strength.

Benefits of unity. "Behold, how good and how pleasant it is for brethren to dwell together in unity!" (Psalm 133:1). By working together in a fellowship that operates with biblical accountability and authority, we enjoy God's protection, blessing, and guidance. Good organization promotes evangelism and outreach. It facilitates joint efforts, the pooling of financial resources, and the pooling of talent. It reinforces beliefs and convictions. It enables missionary work, as in the early church, and it enables each local assembly to take part in the great commission.

Organization offers protection against the infiltration of Satan and sin. As in the early church, it provides a means of knowing those who labor among us and distinguishing between true and false leadership. It provides a means of having fellowship with people of like precious faith, of establishing biblical qualifications for leadership, and of maintaining guidelines for Christian living.

When faced with new situations, the body can seek the leading of the Spirit, as the church did in Acts 15. "In the multitude of counsellers there is safety" (Proverbs

11:14). “Two are better than one . . . and a threefold cord is not quickly broken” (Ecclesiastes 4:9-12). God honors the collective decision of His church, and He can use this method to implement His will (Acts 15:28).

All believers, including ministers, need to operate within a system of godly authority and fellowship. A large fellowship helps to keep local groups in the mainstream of God’s will. The diversity of viewpoints keeps the whole group in balance. It also keeps the whole body invigorated and progressive in outlook.

Let us submit to God’s appointed authority and leadership. Ministers should be the best example of all. “Neither as being lords over God’s heritage, but being ensamples to the flock” (I Peter 5:3). No one is exempt from authority, but everyone can profit from encouragement, counsel, advice, warning, and if necessary, rebuke. The church as a whole will profit from strong leadership that safeguards and promotes precious truths.

CHAPTER

13

Fellowship and Alliances

And have no fellowship with the unfruitful works of darkness, but rather reprove them (Ephesians 5:11).

Be ye not unequally yoked together with unbelievers (II Corinthians 6:14).

Fellowship with the world. Separation from the world is a key component of holiness. (See chapters 1 and 6.) In previous chapters we have seen that holiness involves separation from worldly practices and things that defile us. Now we will consider circumstances in which holiness requires separation from certain types of people.

The Bible instructs us about the kind of company we keep and the kind of friends we have. "Make no friendship with an angry man; and with a furious man thou shalt not go: lest thou learn his ways, and get a snare to thy soul" (Proverbs 22:24-25). "Be not deceived: evil communications corrupt good manners" (I Corinthians 15:33). "Bad company corrupts good character" (NIV). "The friendship of the world is enmity with God" (James 4:4).

These verses reveal that holiness involves our friendships. Inevitably, the attitudes and spirits of our companions will influence us. If we associate closely with evil people, we will be adversely affected.

This does not mean that we should avoid all association with sinners. When Jesus was criticized for eating with tax collectors and sinners, He explained that it was His mission to save them (Luke 5:30-32). Likewise, if we expect to win souls, we must associate with them. The best way to win souls is to be a friend.

In addition, some interaction with sinners is necessary as part of daily life. Although we are not of the world, we are still in the world. Paul wrote that believers should not keep company with fornicators but explained that he did not mean we must avoid all associations with fornicators in the world (I Corinthians 5:9-10).

Even so, we must draw a line at some point. According to Ephesians 5:11, we cannot have fellowship with works of darkness. We cannot endorse or participate in sin. When worldly acquaintances and friends begin to indulge in their worldly activities, we must politely withdraw.

For this reason, there will always be a certain barrier between a Christian and unsaved friends. They can be good friends, but only to a certain point. There will always be some activities in which the Christian will not participate, and there will always be some things that the sinner will not understand about the Christian's experience.

Christians also need to be careful not to become

identified with sinful activities or worldly attitudes by reason of their associations. As the saying goes, "A man is known by the company he keeps." "Birds of a feather flock together."

In short, Christians will associate with sinners to some extent in order to befriend them, win them to the Lord, and live normally in this world. However, Christians cannot participate in sinful activities or allow themselves to be identified too closely with worldliness.

In addition to these general considerations, the Bible gives specific directions in two areas. First, we must not have fellowship with people who call themselves Christians but who live in the type of notorious sins discussed below. Second, we must not become unequally yoked together with unbelievers.

Fellowship with sinners in the church. Several parables of Jesus in Matthew 13 reveal that Christendom, or the outward church, contains both sinners and saints. The kingdom of heaven is like a field of wheat and tares, a mustard tree with all manner of birds nesting in it, a quantity of meal with leaven in it, and a net filled with all kinds of fish. The point is that professing Christianity contains many people who are not truly Christian in their faith and conduct.

The visible church potentially contains false prophets, false apostles, false teachers, and teachers of demonic doctrines (I Timothy 4:1; II Peter 2:1; Revelation 2:2). Indeed, we can compare much of modern Christianity to the Laodicean church in Revelation 3:14-22. Many congregations have extensive assets, beautiful buildings, talented choirs, and elaborate rituals, but often Christ is on the outside, knocking for admittance. Many organizations and religious traditions do not proclaim the full gospel, and many adherents are not born-again believers. Finally, in every group there are some who do not live what they profess. In certain cases, the church has the authority to judge such people and remove them from the church. (See chapter 12.)

When people are judged and removed from fellowship according to God's Word, we should not have fellowship with them. If we do, we place our personal judgment ahead of the God-given authority and judgment of the church. One purpose of this judgment is to separate the evil from the good—to remove the old leaven (yeast) before it affects the whole batch of dough (I Corinthians 5:6-7). If we continue to associate with such people, we will harm ourselves.

We will also harm those who have been removed from fellowship, for another purpose of disciplinary action is to help wrongdoers see their sinful state and bring them to repentance. If instead we comfort them, they will learn to be insincere and hypocritical. Often, they simply change churches or organizations without repenting, making restitution, asking forgiveness, or meeting biblical qualifications. Those who help them to evade scriptural discipline are condoning their sin, are supporting rebellion, and will be accountable to God (II John 11).

The Bible lists several types of people who should be removed from fellowship if they persist in their sins. Even if the church has not officially judged the matter, we should not associate closely with professing believers who manifest these sins. Let us look at some important passages of Scripture that give us instructions in this matter.

But now I have written unto you not to keep company, if any man that is called a brother be a fornicator, or covetous, or an idolater, or a railer, or a drunkard, or an extortioner; with such an one no not to eat (I Corinthians 5:11).

This verse speaks of those who claim to be members of our church but who live in hypocrisy with regard to certain open sins. We are strongly admonished not even to eat with such people. However, we can still have contact with people in the world who fall under the same categories, because they are not living in hypocrisy (I Corinthians 5:9-10).

Now we command you, brethren, in the name of our Lord Jesus Christ, that ye withdraw yourselves from every brother that walketh disorderly, and not after the tradition which he received of us. . . . For we hear that there are some which walk among you disorderly, working not at all, but are busybodies. . . . And if any man obey not our word by this epistle, note that man, and have no company with him, that he may be ashamed (II Thessalonians 3:6, 11, 14).

Now I beseech you, brethren, mark them which cause divisions and offences contrary to the doctrine which ye have learned; and avoid them (Romans 16:17).

If any man teach otherwise, and consent not to wholesome words, even the words of our Lord Jesus Christ, and to the doctrine which is according to godliness; he is proud, knowing nothing, but doting about questions and strifes of words, whereof cometh envy, strife, railings, evil surmisings, perverse disputings of men of corrupt minds, and destitute of the truth, supposing that gain is godliness: from such withdraw thyself (I Timothy 6:3-5).

Whosoever transgresseth, and abideth not in the doctrine of Christ, hath not God. He that abideth in the doctrine of Christ, he hath both the Father and the Son. If there come any unto you, and bring not this doctrine, receive him not into your house, neither bid him God speed: for he that biddeth him God speed is partaker of his evil deeds (II John 9-11).

Now let us examine the people who are described in these passages of Scripture.

- *Fornicators*: those who live in sexual immorality. (See chapter 9.)
- *Covetous*: those who manifest greed. A person may covet money, clothes, or even a position in the church. This attitude usually displays itself in the form of jealousy, hatred, or speaking evil of others. Such a person may also be guilty of fraud or theft.
- *Idolaters*: worshipers of images or false gods.
- *Railers*: revilers; those who habitually abuse others by words. This attitude is expressed by speaking evil of others, destructive criticism, and slander. (See chapter 4.)
- *Drunkards*: those who get drunk (intoxicated by

alcohol or drugs).

- *Extortioners*: those who obtain money, favors, behavior, or promises by force, fraud, blackmail or other undue pressure. (See chapter 11.) More generally, this word could refer to swindlers.
- *Those who walk disorderly*: those who live contrary to the fundamental guidelines for Christian living as revealed in God's Word. II Thessalonians 3 makes specific application to *those who are lazy and refuse to work*. Although they are able to earn an honest living, they refuse to provide for themselves but expect the church to take care of them. Moreover, they are *busybodies*—people who meddle in the personal affairs of others and in matters outside their authority. (See chapter 3.)
- *False teachers*: those who teach false doctrine, contrary to the fundamental tenets of the faith as revealed in God's Word. Romans, I Timothy, and II John all address this situation. On many points we can have differences of opinion and even differences of scriptural interpretation, but we must unite around the essentials of the faith. As revealed by defining passages of Scripture, these essentials include the authority of Scripture; worship of the one true God; the full deity and full humanity of Jesus Christ; the atoning death, burial, and resurrection of Jesus Christ; salvation by grace through faith; the new birth experience of repentance, water baptism in the name of Jesus Christ, and the baptism of the Holy Spirit; loving God and loving one another; holiness of life both inwardly and outwardly; expressive, heartfelt worship; miracles and gifts of the

Spirit; the second coming of Christ; the resurrection of the dead; and eternal judgment of the righteous and unrighteous. (See Mark 12:28-32; Acts 2:1-47; I Corinthians 2:1-5; 15:1-4; II Timothy 3:15-17; Hebrews 6:1-2.)

In Romans, the test of true and false doctrine is "the doctrine which ye have learned," that is, the teaching of the apostles. In I Timothy, it is "the words of our Lord Jesus Christ" and "the doctrine which is according to godliness." This passage continues by explaining that false teachers typically manifest or cause envy, strife, railing, evil surmisings, and perverse disputings.

- *Envy* is a feeling of resentment and discontent aroused by desire for the position, responsibilities, or possessions of others. (See chapter 3.)
- *Strife* is dissension, contention, struggle for superiority, division into factions, or personal clashes. It includes the sowing of discord. (See chapter 4.)
- *Railing*, or reviling, is harsh and abusive speech. (See chapter 4.)
- *Evil surmising*, or evil suspicion, involves jumping to conclusions, assuming evil things, or assigning evil motives to others. People with this spirit often accuse an innocent person based on some insignificant thing they have seen or heard (or think they saw or heard). It is displayed by destructive criticism and talebearing (slander). (See chapter 4.)
- *Perverse disputing*, or useless wrangling. False teachers instigate conflict where there should be

none.

In II John, the warning against false teachers focuses on "the doctrine of Christ," which in the context of John's epistles is the teaching that God has come in the flesh in the person of Jesus Christ. Those who understand the truth about Jesus Christ will have both the Father and the Son (verse 9), because they will understand that the Son is the revelation of the Father in flesh.

If some deny this truth, we cannot assist their ministry by receiving them into our homes. We cannot even tell them "God speed," meaning "May God prosper you," or "May God give you success," lest we partake of their evil deeds. In other words, we cannot help teachers of false doctrine in their ministry, even to the extent of wishing them success in their endeavor.

In that day, there were no church buildings, so believers met in each other's homes for worship. John did not forbid the kindness and hospitality that we should demonstrate toward everyone, but he warned against letting a teacher of false doctrine come into a home to lead worship or to teach.

There are good reasons why God has commanded us to separate ourselves from the kind of people we have described. They have dangerous attitudes and spirits. If we have close fellowship with those who profess to be believers or even preachers of the gospel, yet they live in an unrepentant state in which they habitually commit or harbor damaging sins—such as fornication, greed, reviling, promotion of false doctrine, and voicing of evil suspicions—then we entertain these spirits. These attitudes or spirits can affect our lives and eventually overcome us. While the Word and Spirit of God will protect us from evil, when we have fellowship with such persons we step out from under the umbrella of God's authority and protection and make ourselves susceptible.

Unequally yoked with unbelievers. "Do not be unequally yoked together with unbelievers. For what fellowship has righteousness with lawlessness? And what communion has light with darkness? And what accord has Christ with Belial? Or what part has a believer with an unbeliever? And what agreement has the temple of God with idols? For you are the temple of the living God. As God has said: 'I will dwell in them and walk among them. I will be their God, and they shall be My people.' Therefore, 'Come out from among them and be separate, says the Lord. Do not touch what is unclean, and I will receive you. I will be a Father to you, and you shall be My sons and daughters, says the LORD Almighty'" (II Corinthians 6:14-18, NKJV).

Righteousness and lawlessness are opposites and cannot be brought together in harmony. The same is true of light and darkness, Christ and Belial (a title for Satan meaning "worthless one"), a believer and an unbeliever, the temple of God (our bodies) and idols. For this reason, we are to separate ourselves from the unclean things of this world, and we are not to become unequally yoked with unbelievers. If we obey this command, we have the promise that the Lord will be our God, dwell in us, receive us, and be our Father.

To be yoked means to be joined together or closely united. In its original usage, the word *yoked* describes animals such as oxen that are paired and fastened together for work. *Webster's Dictionary* gives the following examples of relationships that are analogous to yoking: bondage, servitude, brotherhood, and marriage. It defines a yokefellow as a companion, partner, associate, husband, or wife. The yoke relationship refers to a close, intimate union in which one person can drastically affect or influence another, in which one person can speak or act for another, and in which there is a sharing of responsibility. The most obvious example that affects us today is marriage. In certain cases, business partnerships and fraternal organizations may come under this definition also.

Marriage is certainly a yoke relationship, because two human beings cannot enter into a closer, more intimate relationship. If this verse does not refer to marriage, then it is impossible to think of a situation in which it would apply. Marriage is a lifelong bond, and God views the couple as a single unit, except in matters of individual salvation. A Christian is free to marry, but only in the Lord—that is, to another Christian (I Corinthians 7:39).

An employer-employee relationship is not a yoke but a relationship of superior to subordinate that either party can terminate. A joint business venture or a partnership can be a yoke if both partners have equal control and are bound by the actions of the other. A fraternal organization can be a yoke depending on how the members are pledged to help each other. A secret society bound by oath is a yoke.

Definition of a believer. A believer is not just one who merely confesses or mentally assents. The biblical proof of belief is obedience to the Word of God (I John 2:3; 5:1-3). A lack of faith results in a lack of obedience (Romans 10:16). Believing is a process that begins with the hearing of the Word of God and continues throughout a Christian's walk with God. In the New Testament, the mark of a believer is to experience the plan of salvation and bear the fruit of the Spirit. (See Acts 2:38; Galatians 5:22-23.)

According to Jesus, a true believer will repent of sins, be baptized, and receive the Holy Spirit. (See Mark 1:15; Mark 16:16; John 7:37-39.) When Cornelius and his household "believed on the Lord Jesus Christ," they received the Holy Spirit with the initial sign of speaking in tongues, and they were baptized in the name of Jesus Christ (Acts 10:44-48; 11:17).When the Philippian jailer and his household believed, they were immediately baptized, even though it was around midnight, and they received an experience that caused them to rejoice (Acts 16:31-33).

It is possible to believe in Jesus to some extent but not to receive the fullness of salvation. Examples are the demons (James 2:19), many people in Jerusalem (John 2:23-25), many religious leaders (John 12:42), many miracle workers (Matthew 7:21-23), Cornelius before Peter's sermon (Acts 10:1-6; 11:14), Simon the magician (Acts 8:13, 20-23), and the Samaritans before the arrival of Peter and John (Acts 8:12, 16). In other words, people are not believers in the full New Testament sense just because they claim to believe or just because they have some understanding and acceptance of Jesus. They must have the correct foundation (Matthew 7:21-23), and they must obey God's plan of salvation.

In short, we should not become yoked together with people simply because they call themselves Christians. We must have the same foundation (fundamental doctrine), the same experience of salvation, and the same basic commitment to living a holy life.

Old Testament examples. Becoming yoked with unbelievers leads to compromise with the world. In every age, God has demanded separation from the world. (See chapters 1 and 6.)

Abraham was called out from his country, his kindred, and his father's house (Genesis 12:1). He made plans so that Isaac would not marry a pagan wife, and Isaac did the same for Jacob (Genesis 24:2-3; 27:46; 28:2). Esau grieved his parents by marrying unbelievers (Genesis 26:34-35). God told the Israelites to avoid pagan customs and marriages with unbelieving nations (Deuteronomy 7:3). Balaam shrewdly advised the Moabites to use intermarriage and idolatry as a means to destroy Israel (Numbers 25:1-3; 31:16). Samson's downfall was Philistine women (Judges 14:2-3; 16:4-5), and Solomon's pagan wives caused him to sin (I Kings 11:4-8). Several times God cleansed Israel of unholy marriages before He could use them as a nation (Numbers 25; Ezra 10; Nehemiah 13:23-31).

Thus, the teaching of II Corinthians 6 is another application of the principle of separation. It is not a new concept but a basic principle throughout God's Word.

Marriage. Christians should not marry unbelievers—those who are not saved. If they do, they are disobedient to God's Word. Nor should Christians marry those who merely profess to be Christians. They should choose partners who share the same basic experience, belief, and lifestyle. Otherwise, they are subjecting themselves to a life of conflict or compromise.

Ministers should only perform marriages that meet biblical standards. They can marry two unbelievers because they are equally yoked. But if they marry an unbeliever to a believer, they are endorsing an action that is contrary to God's Word.

If a believer is married to an unbeliever, it is God's will for them to remain married. God honors the marriage vow and is not in favor of it being broken (I Corinthians 7:10-13, 39). In such a case the believing spouse sanctifies the unbeliever (verse 14). In other words, the relationship is lawful, and the believer has a spiritual influence on the unbeliever and on the children. In this situation, the believer's duty is to try to win the unbelieving spouse through prayer and a holy life (I Peter 3:1-2).

Some think that marrying an unbeliever is a good way to win that person to the Lord. But we cannot expect good results by disobeying the Word of God. Usually, when unbelievers are sincerely interested in God, they will be baptized and receive the Holy Spirit before the marriage takes place. In most cases of a believer marrying an unbeliever, the unbeliever never comes to the Lord. It is more common for the believing spouse to backslide or to compromise important beliefs.

At the least, the believing spouse will be forced into certain accommodations in order to maintain the marriage. The believer will not be free to do God's perfect will in all things and will have less time to devote to God. It is also likely that some of the children will follow the example of the unbelieving spouse.

Those who are in this situation should be faithful to God and trust Him. In many cases, they are able to win their family through their godly lifestyle and intercessory prayer. Those who come into the church after marriage should have great faith that God will save the rest of their family, but those who are already in the church should not marry outside the church.

Dating. Since it is not God's will to marry outside the faith, then it is not God's will to establish a dating relationship outside the faith. Young adults typically marry someone they have dated. They should not establish with an unbeliever the kind of close relationship that might result in marriage.

Some casual contact, fellowship, or going out together as part of a Christian group may be permissible and may even help win someone to the Lord. Once a dating relationship is established, however, the possibility of winning the unbeliever is subordinated to the attraction between the two. At this point the Christian will have to expend great effort just to maintain his or her own convictions and will be vulnerable to temptation. It will usually be difficult to uphold Christian standards of conduct in dating.

Then there is the possibility that love will develop, causing the Christian to face the agonizing decision of breaking up, waiting for a conversion that may never occur, or going against God's will by marrying an unbeliever. Christians should not expose themselves to these tensions, even if they are spiritually strong and confident. "Wherefore let him that thinketh he standeth take heed lest he fall" (I Corinthians 10:12). If we invite problems in this manner we cannot rely on God's promise that He will not put on us more than we can bear. Nor can we rely on His promise that all things will work together for good. While we are getting sidetracked in this manner, we may miss God's perfect will.

Leaders need to give advice in this matter according to the Word of God, not according to their hopes in a particular situation. While some situations turn out well in the end, it is only by the grace of God. But the end does not justify the means. We cannot encourage people to take a risk contrary to God's Word.

If we want God's blessings, we should follow His Word and seek His will. As we pray and consecrate ourselves to Him, He will direct our lives. If we first seek God and His righteousness, then He will take care of our needs (Matthew 6:33).

CHAPTER

14

Worship, Emotions, and Music

Worship the L*ORD in the beauty of holiness* (I Chronicles 16:29; Psalm 29:2; 96:9).

Worship him in spirit and in truth (John 4:24).

True worship. Worship is an integral part of holiness, and holiness is an essential ingredient of worship. The truest form of worship is obedience, not sacrifice or offerings (I Samuel 15:22). God will reject worship if it is not coupled with a desire for holiness. (See Amos 5:21-27; Malachi 1:10.) God accepts worship that comes from a sincere heart and a surrendered will. We are to worship God both in spirit and in truth.

The rest of this book discusses the way we worship God in our everyday lives. This chapter focuses on worshiping Him with outward expression and emotions.

Emotions and expression. Biblical worship affects

every aspect of the human being. God asks that we love Him with all our heart, soul, mind, and strength (Mark 12:30). These words cover the emotional, spiritual, intellectual, and physical dimensions of human life. All are involved in worship. Ultimately, it is our will, not our emotions or intellect, that gives commitment and stability to our worship.

Some say that emotion and physical expression should play a minor role in worship. Others say that they are not emotional or demonstrative by nature. While people do have different temperaments, true worship involves all aspects of a person, including the emotional component that exists in everyone.

God is a God of emotions. Throughout the Bible He displayed emotions such as love, joy, sorrow, and anger. Jesus, as God manifested in flesh, wept at the tomb of His friend Lazarus and over the city of Jerusalem (John 11:35; Luke 19:41). He "rejoiced in spirit" over the good report of the seventy disciples (Luke 10:21). The Greek word here means to exult or to leap for joy.

We are created in the image of God (Genesis 1:27), and like Him, we have emotions. Some claim that they are not emotional and therefore prefer formality in worship. Everyone expresses emotions in other areas of life, however. The supposedly unemotional will caress and embrace their loved ones, or lose their temper at a slight provocation, or shout at football games, or vehemently assert their rights, or pout when they do not get their way. The fact is that we are emotional beings. Emotion plays a part in every aspect of our lives, and therefore we should not exclude it from worship. It is not the only component, but it is an important component.

Emotion leads to physical expression. It is impossible to feel intense emotion without expressing it in some way. By itself, physical expression is only a small part of worship. Indeed, "bodily exercise profiteth little" (I Timothy 4:8). Yet physical demonstration is a natural and inevitable result of emotion. When motivated by a sincere heart that has been touched by God, physical expression is an important part of worship.

Both testaments demonstrate this truth. The psalmist said, "I will praise the LORD with my whole heart, in the assembly of the upright, and in the congregation" (Psalm 111:1). Here are some examples of appropriate praise in the congregation, according to Psalms: lifting of hands (141:2), singing and playing musical instruments (33:2-3), making a joyful noise (95:1-2), clapping hands (47:1), and dancing (149:3). We are to make a joyful noise, to make a loud noise, to rejoice, and to sing praises (Psalm 98:4). For those who are reluctant to praise God in this manner, the psalmist exhorted, "Let everything that hath breath praise the LORD. Praise ye the LORD" (150:6).

Examples of worship. At the dedication of the Temple, Solomon prayed while standing and lifting his hands and also while kneeling (I Kings 8:22, 54). When the ark of God returned to Jerusalem, David was so overjoyed that he took off his kingly outer garment and danced in the sight of all Israel. "David danced before the LORD with all his might," and came shouting and leaping. His wife, Michal, despised him when she saw this, because she thought he was degrading himself in front of all the people. When she rebuked him, he vowed to act even more "vile" and "base." As a result of this incident, Michal bore no child for the rest of her life. (See II Samuel 6:14-23.)

David was an Oriental king who had great power and dignity, yet he worshiped freely when the ark, symbolic of the presence of God, returned to Jerusalem. Why should not we do the same when the manifested presence of God comes into our midst? (See also Nehemiah 8:6-9; 9:3-5.)

We find the same type of worship in the New Testament. When the 120 believers received the Holy Spirit on the Day of Pentecost, they rejoiced and made so much noise that a large crowd soon gathered. The Spirit-filled believers were so demonstrative that the onlookers thought they were drunk (Acts 2:13). Their lips and tongues were moving in strange ways. As with drunken people generally, there were probably a variety of manifestations such as dancing, shouting, laughing, crying, and staggering. Some probably looked as if they had passed out. If we have received the same Spirit, should our experience be any different?

When the lame man was healed, he entered the Temple walking, leaping, and praising (Acts 3:8). When John saw the Lord on the island of Patmos, he fell down as if he were dead (Revelation 1:17). Paul on the road to Damascus and the jailer in Philippi both trembled under the convicting power of God (Acts 9:6; 16:29-30). When Peter repented of his denial of Christ, he wept bitterly (Luke 22:62). The tax collector struck his breast in repentance (Luke 18:13), and a sinful woman wept tears of repentance, joy, and love when she met Jesus (Luke 7:37-47). Paul wept over the letters of rebuke that he had to send to the churches (II Corinthians 2:4).

When the early church gathered, they prayed aloud together and the whole building was shaken by the power of God (Acts 4:24-31). The Epistles refer to groaning in the Spirit (Romans 8:26), praying and singing in the spirit (I Corinthians 14:15), and lifting of hands (I Timothy 2:8). In the last passage, we see the wide scope of demonstrative worship and its connection with holiness: "I will therefore that men pray every where, lifting up holy hands, without wrath and doubting."

These examples show that sincere worshipers of God express their emotions freely. Not everyone worships or responds in exactly the same way. Some will show more outward emotion, but everyone will be affected. There is room for spontaneity, freedom, and diversity of worship based on individual personality and culture. When God touches us, we will express ourselves. When we are truly sorry for our sins or truly burdened for the lost, we will likely shed tears. When we receive great victory, we will likely shout, dance, laugh, run, or leap for joy.

Quenching the Spirit. "Quench not the Spirit" (I Thessalonians 5:19). Sometimes the Spirit is quenched by formality and unscriptural traditions. Some people worship freely during revival services but revert to formality the rest of the time, especially on Sunday mornings. Many are bound by preconceived ideas of how God will move and by traditional rituals of worship.

On the other hand, we should not try to force a move of God by sensationalism. When God is in control, our worship will edify, or build up, the body (I Corinthians 14:26). It will not bring confusion but peace. The worship may be exuberant and demonstrative, yet all things will be done decently and in order (I Corinthians 14:33, 40). As the leader of the congregation, the pastor will keep scriptural order. There will be no place for hypocrisy or fleshly exaltation in worship.

The church is a place where we meet God. We should not hold back our emotions from God when we meet Him. If believers are free to worship, praise, weep, laugh, and rejoice in the house of God, then it will be easy for people to repent of their sins and receive the Holy Spirit. People rarely receive spiritual blessings or the baptism of the Holy Spirit in an unemotional, formal, restrained atmosphere.

God asks us to surrender the whole self to Him in worship. As we let the Spirit have His way, He will guide us in true worship. We do not need to be embarrassed about showing our emotions, for God is the one who created us as emotional beings. We should let God use our emotions to minister to us.

"Where the Spirit of the Lord is, there is liberty" (II Corinthians 3:17). The Spirit gives each of us the freedom to worship and respond to God's presence in our own way.

Music in worship. The right kind of music can help drive away worries and evil thoughts and can bring peace, encouragement, and closeness to God. As the Psalms indicate, music is an important means of worship. In fact, the book was a hymnal for Israel. We come before God's presence with singing, enter into His gates with thanksgiving, and enter into His courts with praise (Psalm 100). Many passages in the Psalms admonish us to worship with singing and with musical instruments. Psalm 150 lists the following instruments used in worship: trumpet, psaltery (a stringed instrument), harp, timbrel (tambourine or drum), stringed instrument, organ (a wind instrument), loud cymbal, and high-sounding cymbal.

The music of David soothed King Saul and helped

drive away evil spirits that troubled him (I Samuel 16:23). After David became king, he appointed musicians to minister in the house of the Lord (I Chronicles 6:31-47). He appointed singers, psaltery players, harpists, and cymbalists to praise the Lord before the ark (I Chronicles 15:16). There were four thousand musicians including 288 highly trained and skilled in song (I Chronicles 23:5; 25:7). We also read of Jeduthun, who prophesied with a harp (I Chronicles 25:3).

When Solomon dedicated the Temple, he arranged for the trumpets and singers to lift up their voices in praises and thanksgiving, together with cymbals and other instruments of music. When they did this with one accord, the glory of God filled the house. His presence was so strong that the priests could not stand to minister (II Chronicles 5:13-14).

When King Jehoshaphat of Judah asked the prophet Elisha to declare the counsel of God, Elisha first asked for a musician to come. "And it came to pass, when the minstrel played, that the hand of the LORD came upon him" (II Kings 3:15). Afterward, Elisha was able to reveal the plan of God, which gave victory over the Moabites. Music prepared Elisha's heart and set the stage for the moving of God's Spirit.

Jehoshaphat himself knew how powerful worship and music could be. Once, when he faced a battle against Ammon and Moab, he appointed singers unto the Lord to praise the beauty of holiness. When they began to sing, the Lord destroyed the enemy (II Chronicles 20:21-22). God began to move when His people began to sing and worship.

Jesus and His disciples sang a hymn at the Last Supper (Matthew 26:30). When Paul and Silas were beaten and jailed at Philippi, they prayed and sang praises at midnight. God responded by sending an earthquake to free them, and as a result they were able to baptize the jailer.

The New Testament instructs us to worship God with music. "Speaking to yourselves in psalms and hymns and spiritual songs, singing and making melody in your heart to the Lord" (Ephesians 5:19). "Teaching and admonishing one another in psalms and hymns and spiritual songs, singing with grace in your hearts to the Lord" (Colossians 3:16). "Psalms" undoubtedly refers to songs from the Book of Psalms, while "hymns and spiritual songs" refers to other gospel songs. In Greek, "making melody" has the connotation of playing a musical instrument. Those who do not believe in worshiping God with a joyful noise, clapping of hands, raising of hands, dancing, and playing of musical instruments would have a difficult time singing all the psalms that recommend these forms of worship. New Testament believers did not have any such qualms, for they used the same forms of worship as in the Psalms.

The New Testament endorses both singing with the spirit (singing in tongues) and singing with the understanding (I Corinthians 14:15). Singing should be an important part of our worship services and our everyday lives (I Corinthians 14:26; James 5:13).

Since music can be such a powerful element of worship, in church services we must employ it primarily for worship rather than entertainment. Many mistakenly believe that church is a stage, the congregation is the audience, the musicians are the performers, and God is backstage giving cues. Actually, the people of the congregation are the performers (worshipers), the musicians give cues, and God is the audience.

In church, the primary goal of singers and musicians should be to worship God from the heart, creating music that He is pleased to hear. Their second function is to create an atmosphere of worship that will encourage the congregation to worship and usher them into the presence of God. Many people have consecrated their lives through the inspiration of anointed singing.

Thus, musicians, singers, and worship leaders have a great responsibility. They can make or break a service. They should fast and pray that God would use them to bless the service. Just as they practice and prepare to make their songs beautiful, they should pray for God to anoint them and use them in a spiritual way. We do not need people who merely want to display their talents, but we need people who want to worship God and who want to inspire the audience to worship.

While it is good for musical groups to sound polished and professional and to have the latest equipment, they should put anointing above talent, and worship above entertainment. It is good to hear a group with beautiful harmony and instrumentation, but it is most important to be able to worship and to feel God's presence while they sing. Some groups may be suitable for a concert but not ideal for a worship service.

Since singers and musicians promote worship in the congregation, they need to be good examples of Christianity. The congregation should be able to see their godly lifestyle and feel their sincerity. True worship is hindered when the singers and musicians do not truly worship, when they perform for self-exaltation, or when they do not endeavor to live a holy life.

Singing and playing in church is a privilege. Those who have musical talent should use it for God. They have an opportunity to worship and thank Him for their ability. For this reason, we typically do not pay singers, choir members, and musicians (unless their occupation is being a part-time or full-time music director). Doing so could rob them of their privilege of worshiping God.

Congregational singing is a form of worship, and it affords an excellent opportunity for people to be blessed. Thus, emcees and leaders of musical worship need to be led by the Spirit and need to have a burden for the service. Their job is to inspire worship, to help people open their hearts, and to prepare them for the preaching of the Word of God. They should feel liberty to follow the moving of the Spirit—to sing a chorus over again, to change songs, to sing a song they had not previously planned. Sometimes God uses a particular song in a service to reach an individual or to lead that service into a new dimension. The service leader should make plans in advance but remain sensitive to the Spirit at all times and mindful of the direction of the pastor.

We often sing short, simple choruses, because they are easy to understand and learn, enabling the congregation to focus on the Lord. It is helpful to have a variety of songs that can evoke true worship and create the atmosphere appropriate for each service.

Many different types of songs can be appropriate for worship, depending on the needs and spirit of the service and the needs and cultural background of the congregation. A congregation with people of various backgrounds and cultures should have a musical program that fits a variety of needs and tastes.

There are times to sing a new song to the Lord (Psalm 96:1). Some songs may not appeal to our personal musical tastes, but they may appeal to others and thus may be helpful in worship. Some styles may be good for some cultural groups but may seem insincere or out of place when used by others. In general, musical forms of worship will to a great extent follow the musical styles of the culture and the age. Regardless of musical style, it is important to worship God sincerely and to seek His presence rather than merely a good feeling.

While a variety of musical styles is good, we should not use music that appeals directly and primarily to sensuality. For example, there is a danger in using some kinds of R&B (rhythm and blues) and rock, because these styles can easily arouse emotions and desires that are incompatible with worship and praise.

Modern music. Christians can enjoy songs and music that are not religiously oriented. At the same time, we should use care when considering the music of the world. Not all of it is compatible with Christian values.

Some songs are inappropriate because of the lyrics, and this problem exists in every secular musical style. Some popular music is relaxed and easygoing, but the words are suggestive of fornication. Much of country and western music dwells heavily on unwholesome themes such as adultery, fornication, divorce, and drinking. Genres such as rock, hip-hop, rap, and R&B are noted for their frequent glorification of lust, illicit sex, drugs, vulgar speech, rebellion, mysticism, and even satanism.

Music has power to influence us subtly and even to captivate our minds. For instance, a song can become lodged in our minds and repeat itself over and over, no matter how much we try to forget it. If it is a song of praise, we can receive a wonderful blessing, but if the song is inappropriate then it can vex our spirits. Thus, if a song comes on the radio that glorifies sin, we should turn it off.

Some types of music can be unwholesome in themselves. For example, some secular styles noted above can cause physiological changes in the human body, affecting the pituitary and sex glands. A heavy beat can stir up the emotions, including the sex drive. Hard rock music can increase tension, stress, disorientation, and loss of self-control. This type of influence explains the actions of performers and audience at worldly concerts and the motions of dancers. In short, some music excites the listeners physically and psychologically, but not in a godly way. We must be careful not to rely upon this type of music to promote worship, or to substitute such responses for worship.

Music can be used both for worship and for personal enjoyment. In church services, we must be careful to emphasize its role as worship instead of entertainment. In our personal lives, we must guard against worldliness that can influence us through certain kinds of music.

CHAPTER

15

Worldly Pleasures

Love not the world, neither the things that are in the world. If any man love the world, the love of the Father is not in him (I John 2:15).

Abstain from all appearance of evil (I Thessalonians 5:22).

Guidelines. In the twenty-first century, we encounter many circumstances that first-century believers did not face. While no biblical statement specifically addresses these situations, we should identify basic principles of Scripture and learn to apply them to our day. As a body of believers and as individual Christians, we must learn to follow the leading of the Spirit in these cases.

As explained in chapter 8, we have Christian liberty in areas that the Word of God does not specifically cover, but we are to exercise that liberty in a responsible manner. (See Romans 14:1-23; I Corinthians 8:1-13; 10:23-33.)

First, we must follow the convictions God has given us. (See chapter 1 for the need of personal convictions.) At the same time, we should not do anything to cause someone else to misunderstand, stumble, or fall. We should not judge one another or belittle the convictions of others. From the discussion of eating food offered to idols, we discover that some things may be harmless in themselves but are nevertheless unwise because of their effect on someone else. Appearances and associations are important in this regard.

Some things are clearly right, other things are clearly wrong, and some things are questionable. In questionable cases, one guideline to consider is, "Whatsoever is not of faith is sin" (Romans 14:23). This leads us to conclude that if something is doubtful, we should not participate in it.

We can also ask, "What would Jesus do in this case?" "What would we do if Jesus were physically accompanying us or visiting us?" Our objective is not to see how close we can get to the world and still be saved, or how many worldly things we can do and still not be considered a backslider. Rather, we want to do God's will at all times and to be identified with God in the eyes of others. Where there is temptation and a possibility of sin, "it is better to be safe than sorry." Moreover, as we draw closer to God in prayer and dedication, we will not want to do anything to grieve Him or to identify us with the world instead of with Him.

The Bible tells us, "Love not the world" (I John 2:15). Here, "world" means the world system, the value system of unregenerated humans—the attitudes, desires, loves, cares, and priorities of sinful flesh. Let us examine this concept in terms of worldly amusement, worldly atmosphere, and worldly appearance.

Amusement. There is nothing wrong with pleasure and enjoyment as such. We do not advocate the idea that something is wrong or suspect because it gives pleasure. God created our minds and bodies with the capacity to have pleasure, both alone and with each other. Jesus came that we might have life and have it more abundantly (John 10:10), which connotes an exuberant, zestful, enjoyable life.

On the other hand, humanity has often placed too much emphasis on pleasure to the exclusion of God. Anything that prevents us from doing God's will is wrong. Anything that interferes with regular church attendance, prayer, and Bible reading is not the will of God.

Some pleasures are sinful. "For we ourselves also were sometimes foolish, disobedient, deceived, serving divers lusts and pleasures, living in malice and envy, hateful, and hating one another" (Titus 3:3). Moses chose "rather to suffer affliction with the people of God, than to enjoy the pleasures of sin for a season" (Hebrews 11:25).

The Bible warns us that in the last days people will be so caught up in pleasure that they will ignore and neglect God. As in Noah's day, people will be preoccupied with eating, drinking, marrying, and giving in marriage, and therefore will not be prepared when the Lord comes (Matthew 24:37-39). These activities are good in themselves but not when done to the exclusion of God and not when perverted by the world. A key sign of the end times is that "men shall be lovers of their own selves" and "lovers of pleasures more than lovers of God" (II Timothy 3:2, 4).

From these passages, we see that some pleasures

are acceptable but can become wrong when taken to excess. We also see that some worldly pleasures are off limits to Christians.

Atmosphere. Sometimes the world corrupts wholesome and enjoyable activities by a worldly atmosphere. A spirit of lust, pleasure madness, or mob violence has permeated them to such a degree that Spirit-filled Christians are uncomfortable participating in them. Some parties, shows, concerts, spectator sports, and places of amusement are characterized by lewdness, drinking, drug use, violence, obscenity, or gambling. For instance, while there is nothing wrong with eating at a restaurant, Christians avoid some restaurants because they advertise immodestly dressed waitresses as a major part of their appeal.

Attending one such event may not result in the immediate commission of sin, but the atmosphere is not conducive to Christian living. When Christians let their conscience guide them, they feel out of place. If they continue to participate, eventually they will lose spiritual sensitivity. They will not be able to discern the holy from the unholy or right from wrong in these areas.

Unfortunately, it is not always possible to avoid a worldly atmosphere. What was once isolated to certain places of amusement has now permeated our entire society. Simply going to a public park, shopping mall, high school, or college campus may expose us to a degree of lewdness, immodesty, and profanity that we previously did not encounter. In cultures, times, and locales where we can identify a certain type of place or activity that harbors a worldly atmosphere distinctly worse than the community experience at large, then we should abstain from such a place or activity. But when the atmosphere is essentially the same as the typical places we need to frequent into order to live in this world, then a simple prohibition does not have the same effect or value.

In this situation, we must take greater care to follow principles of holiness, to make wise decisions based on individual circumstances, and to trust the sanctifying power of the Holy Spirit. Where sin abounds, grace much more abounds. (See Romans 5:20.) God's grace is sufficient for every circumstance. (See II Corinthians 12:9.) When we do our best to follow godly principles and make godly choices in areas under our control, then we can trust God to protect and preserve us from the evil influence of the world around us.

In sum, God does not expect Christians to remove themselves completely from the world. His plan is to preserve us in holiness while we are still in the world and to send us into the world as witnesses for Him. Thus Jesus said, "I pray not that thou shouldest take them out of the world, but that thou shouldest keep them from the evil. They are not of the world, even as I am not of the world. Sanctify them through thy truth: thy word is truth. As thou hast sent me into the world, even so have I also sent them into the world" (John 17:15-18).

Appearance. In some situations, neither the amusement itself nor the atmosphere is excessively worldly, but participation may still appear worldly in the eyes of others. In these situations, we should take care not to damage our testimony or to cause a stumbling block for others. For example, if we appear to be gambling or drinking an alcoholic beverage, even when we are not, we may project a worldly appearance that is harmful to others. Similarly, if our boss at work asks us to buy cigarettes for her, will onlookers think we participate in or condone smoking?

No list of rules would be sufficient to cover all such situations. Rather, each person must be sensitive to the voice of conscience in this area, being motivated by genuine love for God and for others.

Gambling. Scripture does not speak directly on the subject, but gambling is a combination of worldly amusement, atmosphere, and appearance. It is closely allied with cheating, violence, organized crime, financial ruin, and suffering by innocent families. It can be addictive, as demonstrated by the existence of Gamblers Anonymous.

In essence, gambling is an appeal to greed—an attempt to get something for nothing. It callously disregards that the winner's gain comes from everyone else's loss—often severe loss by individuals and families who cannot afford it.

The Bible teaches us not to come under the power of addictive habits. (See Romans 6:16; I Corinthians 6:12). It teaches to work for what we need, to trust God to supply our needs, to be good stewards of our finances, not to incur debts that we cannot or will not repay, above all to provide for our own families, to treat others as we wish to be treated, and to show compassion for the needy. (See Proverbs 3:9-10; 6:6-8; Matthew 5:42; 6:33; 7:12; Romans 13:8; II Thessalonians 3:10-12; I Timothy 5:8.) It warns us against greed, which it equates with idolatry (Luke 12:15; Colossians 3:5). It warns us that the love of money is the root of all types of evil and admonishes us to be content with our possessions (I Timothy 6:6-10). If we have a desire to improve our lives, we should be willing to work for that goal.

To avoid violation of these scriptural teachings, we avoid gambling. To be consistent and to abstain from all appearance of evil, we avoid all forms of gambling, including betting and lotteries.

Dancing. The primary motivation behind most forms of social dancing in modern Western culture is sexuality, conscious or unconscious. Such dancing frequently arouses lusts between people who are not married to each other, often leading to temptation and sin. For instance, the close physical contact of ballroom dancing can sexually arouse the dancers. In contemporary forms of dancing, the bodily movements can cause sexual excitement. Moreover, modern dancing is often an expression of egotism and exhibitionism, and as such it is not in harmony with the Spirit of God.

Sports. In general, sports can be wholesome activities that promote physical health, fellowship, enjoyment, and character development. When played in a casual, friendly atmosphere, sports such as football, basketball, softball, and soccer are fine. When sports become highly organized in a secular environment, however, several problems can result. We typically see these problems in secular American high schools, colleges, and professional leagues.

- Competitive sports often demand *excessive time and dedication* that take precedence over the players' relationship with God as well as their physical, mental, and spiritual well-being. Playing sports at this level can interfere with church attendance, prayer, and fellowship with God's people. Often it means close fellowship with sinners whose lifestyle and pursuit of pleasure are contrary to Christian principles. One high school student wanted to play football but asked what accommodations could be made when practices conflicted with important church functions. The coach responded, "If you are going to be on this team, then football must be more important than church." Another example of the intense commitment to the detriment of the players is the frequent use of steroids and other substances that are harmful to the body.

- Participants may have to wear *immodest or unisex clothing* that is contrary to biblical teaching. (See chapter 6.) Suggestive clothing may be part of the appeal, as in the case of cheerleaders and some women's sports such as beach volleyball.
- Sometimes sports are conducted in a *worldly atmosphere* that is detrimental to both spectator and player. In the larger games, there can be a spirit of mob violence in which people fight, throw objects, curse, bet, and get drunk. The rivalry can become so intense that it cultivates hatred, evil speech, and malice. Coaches, players, and fans become noted for poor sportsmanship, arrogance, vicious speech, and uncontrolled tempers.
- All too often, the result is to *glorify violence*. In some games, the goal is to injure opponents, and some sports derive much of their popularity from the high degree of violence or the high risk of bodily harm. Boxing exalts violence, as does professional wrestling. Fighting is part of the appeal of hockey, crashes are part of the thrill of racing, and bone-crushing tackles are an important factor in

football. Consequently, some sports cause a large number of injuries and even permanent damage—all in order to satisfy pleasure, much as in the days of the Roman gladiators. On an international level, soccer games are notorious for resulting in riots.

- Modern organized sports tend to *glorify the athletes*, to their own detriment as well as the detriment of society. Some of them flaunt greedy, ostentatious, and immoral lifestyles and become negative role models for youth.
- For many people, sports become *an obsession, an addiction, an idol*—even the equivalent of a religion. Baron Pierre de Coubertin, who inspired recreation of the Olympic Games in 1896, stated, "For me, sport is a religion with church, dogma, ritual."[1] This obsession is manifested in many ways. Fans will sacrifice prayer time, church attendance, and family relationships in order to watch sports programs. Many youth and men may not be able to name the books of the Bible or explain the fundamentals of the faith with Scripture references, but they can recite players, teams, scores, and statistics. In children's leagues, some parents and coaches place great pressure on young children to practice and compete intensely. In too many cases, the result is to take most of the fun out of the sport and to cause physical and emotional damage to developing children.

The attitudes we have described are contrary to Christian values, and Christians feel uncomfortable in such an atmosphere. Experience has shown that, for the reasons we have discussed, a large number of Christians who participate seriously in secular, organized, competitive sports, especially at the higher levels, eventually compromise or abandon their beliefs.

In sum, sports can be wholesome, but they can also be polluted by a sinful world. If sports can be conducted in a wholesome atmosphere, then there is nothing wrong in doing so. By this we mean minimizing the problems stated above, so that crowds and tempers are under control, opponents maintain friendly relations, and everyone displays good sportsmanship. Let us avoid becoming too preoccupied with sports, so that we are not caught up in a worldly spirit.

In all pursuit of sports, games, and other amusements, we desire a Christian atmosphere or at least a family atmosphere in which sin is not blatant. We do not want to create a stumbling block for ourselves or others, and we do not want to bring a reproach upon our church or our Lord. Therefore, we avoid activities that have a sinful atmosphere or an appearance of evil. We should follow both the guidance of the Holy Spirit in our conscience and the advice of Spirit-filled, God-called pastors.

Witchcraft refers to attempts to forecast, influence, or control events or forces by supernatural means. It includes the use of charms, spells, rituals, and invocation of spirits. Of course, we pray to the one true God to ask for His influence and intervention in our lives according to His will, but we should not invoke any other spirits or seek to exercise our own will by supernatural means.

The Bible strongly condemns all forms of witchcraft. The law sentenced witches to death (Exodus 22:18). Deuteronomy 18:9-12 lists nine forbidden activities that are abominations to God. While there is some overlap in meaning, this list covers all witchcraft or sorcery. It tells us that God hates (detests) the activities of the following people:

- *Anyone who practices human sacrifice.*
- *Anyone who practices "divination"* (mystical insight or fortunetelling).
- *"Observer of times"*: someone who is superstitious, observing lucky and unlucky days, signs, and practices. The NIV uses "sorcery," referring to someone who seeks supernatural power by the assistance of spirits.
- *"Enchanter."* The NKJV and NIV translate the Hebrew term as someone who "interprets omens" (prophetic signs).
- *"Witch"*: someone who seeks to exercise supernatural powers by magic or assistance of spirits.
- *"Charmer"*: someone who attempts to cast spells.
- *"Consulter with familiar spirits"*: medium, someone who attempts to contact evil spirits (demons).
- *"Wizard"*: sorcerer. The NKJV and NIV translate the Hebrew word as "spiritist," referring to someone who attempts to contact spirits.
- *"Necromancer"*: someone who attempts to consult the dead.

All abominable, sorcerers, and idolaters will have their part in the lake of fire (Revelation 21:8). Witchcraft is one of the works of the flesh (Galatians 5:19-21).

Paul discerned that a certain girl who was a soothsayer was possessed by "a spirit of divination." He took authority over the spirit and cast it out in the name of

Jesus (Acts 16:16-18). He also organized a public burning in Ephesus in which occult books worth 50,000 pieces of silver were destroyed (Acts 19:18-20).

In modern times, many people have assumed that the practice of witchcraft would diminish, but the opposite is true. There has been a resurgence of all forms of witchcraft in America and around the world, and it is sometimes mixed with Christianity. We are experiencing an increase of interest in satanism, paganism, mysticism, fortunetelling, occult books, horoscopes, and astrological signs. These things are nothing less than a revival of witchcraft inspired by satanic forces.

The practice of *astrology* falls under the condemnation of witchcraft. Astrologers, stargazers, and monthly prognosticators cannot help us; they cannot even deliver themselves from ultimately burning with fire (Isaiah 47:12-15). We are not to be dismayed at the signs of heaven as the heathen are (Jeremiah 10:2). Thus, we should not use horoscopes and zodiac signs to seek advice or predict the future. Astrologers, magicians, and soothsayers failed to reveal God's will to Nebuchadnezzar and to Belshazzar. It took a man of God to give them the true message of God (Daniel 2:27; 5:15).

Since God hates all these practices, and since they are associated with evil spirits, Christians must not participate in anything associated with witchcraft. It is against the will of God to believe in astrology, to consult a horoscope, or to visit a fortuneteller or palm reader. Christians should not use tarot cards, Ouija boards, zodiac signs or the like, even in fun. They open up the mind to the devil and allow him to operate more freely. For the same reason, Christians should not participate in a séance, even in jest. If séance is "successful," it involves contact with an evil spirit.

Those who participate in an Oriental martial art should be careful, since these sports are often associated with mysticism, Eastern philosophy, and spirit worship. They must make sure not to participate in anything associated with paganism or witchcraft.

Yoga and transcendental meditation can be dangerous spiritually. They are based on Hinduism and Buddhism and can open the mind to the world of evil spirits. Many of the words used in such disciplines are actually prayers to pagan gods, and demons receive this worship.

Christians should be cautious about opening the mind to the spirit world. Evil spirits are waiting to influence us and take advantage of us. Many people open themselves to this influence through mind-altering experiences such as using drugs, listening to certain types of worldly music, and meditating in mystical ways. When we pray or speak in tongues, we should always do so by the name and blood of Jesus, focus our minds on God, and maintain some awareness and self-control. The Spirit of God may overwhelm us at times, but He will never violate our human will. The spirit of prophecy is and should be under the control of the prophet (I Corinthians 14:32). Moreover, when we pray in Jesus' name, having faith in His blood, we have assurance the devil cannot intervene in response to that prayer.

Superstition is a related evil that has no place in the mind of a Christian. There are no lucky or unlucky days, numbers, or rituals. A Christian has no reason to regard omens or wear lucky charms. God is in control of our lives, He protects His own, and He works all things together for our good. (See Ephesians 1:11; Psalm 91:9-12; Romans 8:28.) Satan could not touch Job's possessions or his health until God lifted the hedge around Job. Even then, Satan did not have the power to take Job's life (Job 1:9-12). Curses, charms, unlucky portents, or deaths of people in certain places have no power over God, His church, or His children.

Satan's power. Satan is not omnipresent, omniscient, or omnipotent, but he does have power. Some witches, magicians, and fortunetellers can perform wonders by his power. The magicians of Egypt did miracles, but Moses was able to overpower them. There came a point where they were rendered powerless in the face of God's power (Exodus 7:10-12, 22; 8:7, 18-19). Jesus predicted that false prophets would come with great signs and wonders (Matthew 24:24). The "man of sin," or Antichrist, will display power, signs, and lying wonders after the working of Satan (II Thessalonians 2:9). The false prophet of the beast (Antichrist) will call fire from heaven and will cause an image of the beast to speak (Revelation 13:11-15). Demonic spirits will work miracles (Revelation 16:13-14).

These things should not surprise us. Under the law, the test of false prophets was not whether they could perform miracles but whether they worshiped the one true God. If they had a dream, sign, or wonder but turned the people away from God, then they were to be executed (Deuteronomy 13:1-5).

In short, it may be possible for some people to do supernatural works by the power of the devil. God's power is greater, however, and Satan can have no power over a Spirit-filled child of God who is living according to His will (John 10:29; James 4:7; I John 4:4). Demons cannot be cast out by holy water, signs, crosses, incantations, or rituals, but only by the name of Jesus called in faith (Mark 16:17; Acts 19:13-17).

Many fortunetellers, magicians, mediums, and the like are mere tricksters and imposters, with no supernatural power. They can still fit into the devil's scheme by hoodwinking the credulous, diverting worship from God, and opening people's minds to the occult and demonic.

The word *magic* can refer to witchcraft and sorcery, but it can also refer to innocent tricks based on sleight of hand, optical illusions, mathematical facts, or secret communication between participants. We oppose the former but not the latter. There is nothing wrong with parlor games and stage tricks unless the performers seek a connection with satanic power or seriously present themselves as miracle workers.

Let us avoid all forms of witchcraft, sorcery, and superstition. Since "rebellion is as the sin of witchcraft" (I Samuel 15:23), let us also make sure we do not harbor a rebellious spirit.

Summary. The point of this chapter is not to develop a list of do's and don'ts but to scrutinize every area of our lives. We should guard against worldliness in whatever guise it may appear. We are well equipped to overcome this spirit and to avoid all appearance of evil. The Bible, the indwelling Holy Spirit, godly pastors and teachers, and a tender conscience will work together to guide us in the paths of righteousness if we will yield our lives to their influence, teaching, and leadership.

Note

[1]Frank Deford, “Let the Games Begin,” *National Geographic*, July 1996, 46.

CHAPTER

16

Practical Suggestions

Perfecting holiness in the fear of God (II Corinthians 7:1).

In this book we have covered a wide range of topics and issues that relate to everyday Christian living. Our purpose has not been to establish rules and regulations but to sincerely discover the will of God for our lives. We have tried to give scriptural guidance of practical use in facing the situations of modern life. We trust that we have raised questions, provoked thought, inspired further study of Scripture, and provided at least some answers.

We hope that readers will study the Bible for themselves, decide what they believe and why they believe it, examine their convictions, and develop personal, scriptural convictions. First of all, it is important to place our faith in Jesus Christ, repent of sin, be baptized in Jesus' name, and receive the gift of the Holy Spirit as in Acts 2.

The abiding presence of God will lead, guide, illuminate the Scriptures, and give power to live a holy, overcoming life. We are changed into the image of Christ by the progressive work of the Spirit (II Corinthians 3:18). Without the Spirit, we simply do not have the power to overcome sin and do God's will.

New converts should not be dismayed or frustrated if they do not understand or agree with everything we have presented. The most important thing is to be willing to grow and learn and to sincerely seek the will of God. They will develop holiness in the sight of God as they study the Scriptures, listen to godly preaching and teaching, follow the leading of the Spirit, listen to their conscience, and follow the convictions that develop under God's direction.

It is likely that some readers will disagree on some points. It is possible that they may have a better understanding in some areas. We simply ask for everyone to seek the mind of God with sincerity.

We should not merely adopt the teachings of others (not even the ones in this book), but we should develop our own beliefs through prayer, thought, and study. Instead of merely relying on what others say or do not say, we should ask God to lead us further into His truth. And we should not be afraid to change our views if God is leading us. "Examine yourselves, whether ye be in the faith; prove your own selves" (II Corinthians 13:5). We should never be afraid of what the will of God may mean for us. We will always profit by drawing closer to God and doing His perfect will. We will never lose by living in holiness.

Holiness does not come simply by mental knowledge. It must emanate from within, which is why the Holy Spirit is essential for Christian living. Holiness must be within us, but if it is within us, it will cause changes on the outside. Holiness will change our attitudes, our talk, our appearance, and our actions. If it does not, something is wrong. "Faith, if it hath not works, is dead, being alone" (James 2:17). When we are born again, "old things are passed away; behold, all things are become new" (II Corinthians 5:17). The things we once loved we now hate, and the things we once hated we now love.

General suggestions. We can only maintain holiness by letting the Holy Spirit have control of all areas of life. Regular prayer, church attendance, and Bible study are all necessary. Psalms is a good book to read for praise and worship, Proverbs is full of wisdom and practical advice, the Gospels reveal the example of Christ's life and teaching, and the New Testament Epistles give much practical guidance on Christian living. For important decisions, difficult trials, or strong temptations, both prayer and fasting are beneficial.

As we seek God's will, it is important to listen as He speaks in times of personal devotion and through the leaders He has placed in the church. It is particularly important to heed the teachings and advice of a God-called, Spirit-filled pastor who loves and cares for the flock. It is a good policy to follow the maximum of the personal convictions we have developed through prayerful study of God's Word and the teachings of our pastor as he or she applies God's Word to current circumstances in a practical way.

It is important to follow personal convictions (if they are consistent with Scripture), because God knows our individual strengths and weaknesses and guides us personally in the life of holiness. It is important to follow pastoral teaching, for the sake of unity in the congregation, a clear witness to the community, and personal self-discipline and submission. The test of submission to leadership does not come when we agree completely but when we are unsure or when we disagree. In these situations, we should recognize that the pastor has the authority and responsibility to lead the flock, and that, by virtue of this role, the pastor is more likely to have the mind of God for the congregation than an individual member would. God may want to lead the congregation beyond a minimum standard so that it becomes an example of consecration and a pacesetter of revival.

In addition, having right attitudes and concepts will help us live for God. Below are some practical guidelines that can help us to perfect holiness in our lives.

Twenty practical guidelines.

1. *"Abstain from all appearance of evil"* (I Thessalonians 5:22). "Abstain from every form of evil" (NKJV). If something is evil, has the appearance or form of evil, or tends to evil, avoid it.

2. *When in doubt about something, don't do it.* "Whatsoever is not of faith is sin" (Romans 14:23). Similarly, knowing to do good but refusing to do it is a sin (James 4:17).

3. *Be kind and compassionate* (Ephesians 4:32). Harsh, hateful, or malicious speech and a rebellious attitude are not Christian. If you do not agree with something, express your opinion in an orderly, controlled, Christian way.

4. *Provide for your family.* "If any man provide not for his own, and specially for those of his own house, he hath denied the faith, and is worse than an infidel" (I Timothy 5:8). It may be beneath your dignity to take a certain job, but if you need a job and this is the only one available to support you and your family honestly, then take it.

Some ministers think they should not do manual labor or work on a secular job, but Paul made tents to support himself and his helpers when they needed money. (See Acts 18:3; I Corinthians 4:12.) It is God's will for a church to support its pastor full time if possible. However, no passage of Scripture teaches that it is wrong for ministers to work with their hands. It is wrong if Christians do not try to provide the necessities for their families.

5. *Be an example to the believer first* (I Timothy 4:12). Believers know what God expects of them—how to act, dress, and talk. It is easier to be an example to unbelievers because they usually do not know what God wants and expects. Become an example to believers in word, conduct, love, spirit, faith, and purity. For example, do not scream at others, revile, become belligerent at church business meetings, or display a bad attitude.

6. *Love the teaching of God's Word.* In these last days, many people do not want a doctrinal preacher (II Timothy 4:2-4). They want love and blessings, but all too often they do not want to hear the truth about sin, salvation, and holiness. They will "not endure sound doctrine" but turn from the truth and enjoy "fables" more than the written and preached Word of God. They have "itching ears" and go to preachers who tickle their ears and allow them to satisfy their own lusts.

Do not give in to this spirit. Pastors, do not be people-pleasers but God-pleasers. Saints, do not allow yourselves to be caught up in this last-day attitude. It will rob you of your desire for holiness and your sensitivity to the voice of God.

7. *Don't listen to talebearing.* If some try to gossip about another believer, tell them, "I don't want to hear negative things about my sister. She is a member of our family—the family of God. If there is a problem, talk to someone who has the authority to deal with the problem, but don't involve me."

We are members of one body. When one member hurts, we all hurt. How can we slander or gossip about one another? Instead of gossiping, the Bible tells us to think on things that are true, honest, just, pure, lovely, of good report, virtuous, and praiseworthy (Philippians 4:8).

8. *Seek reconciliation.* If someone has something against you, go to that person to resolve the problem. Before you present yourself to God, seek reconciliation (Matthew 5:23-24). It is carnal to retaliate—to give evil for evil.

9. *Don't become a stumbling block to other believers.* Never be guilty of betraying or discouraging fellow Christians.

Joseph was betrayed by his brothers. Moses was discouraged by fellow Israelites. Jesus died in the house of His friends—betrayed, denied, and forsaken by those closest to Him. Mistreatment by fellow believers brings more discouragement than persecution from the world. Some people in church are fault finders. Usually, they are not very productive themselves and feel guilty or jealous, so they criticize others.

Do not discourage saints by fault finding, a superior attitude, or a reluctance to work. On the contrary, encourage them with the hope that Jesus is coming soon (I Thessalonians 4:18).

10. *Desire spiritual things.* Be content with the physical state in which you find yourself, and focus on spiritual priorities. Make suitable plans and set goals for advancement, but do not be overly concerned with possessions, styles, and luxuries of the world. "For I have learned, in whatsoever state I am, therewith to be content" (Philippians 4:11).

11. *Beware of carnal human reasoning.* "Let no man deceive you with vain words" (Ephesians 5:6). "Beware lest any man spoil you through philosophy and vain deceit, after the tradition of men, after the rudiments of the world, and not after Christ" (Colossians 2:8). Be careful of the words you heed. Be cautious about listening to various religious programs or attending various churches, prayer meetings, and revival services, lest you become confused by conflicting teachings. Know your Bible. Don't be deceived by human traditions and opinions that are contrary to Scripture.

12. *Don't make excuses.* Do not say, "I would be a better Christian if only I lived in Jesus' day, if only I could hear the apostles preach, if only I had been raised in a Christian family, if only I had a better pastor, if only I attended a bigger church." Learn to overcome in your present circumstances. God has promised not to put on you more than you can bear and also to provide a way of escape in every trial or temptation (I Corinthians 10:13). He has promised that His grace would be sufficient (II Corinthians 12:9-10).

In Christ's day, the vast majority rejected Jesus. The multitudes followed Him for miracles and blessings, but they forsook Him when His teaching became challenging. Paul had problems in almost every church he founded. Some criticized, "His letters are weighty and forceful, but in person he is unimpressive and his speaking amounts to nothing" (II Corinthians 10:10, NIV). Because of opposition in the Corinthian church, he was forced to defend his apostleship, handling of finances, and conduct of ministry (II Corinthians 12:11-21).

People typically think "the grass is greener on the other side of the fence." But today is the greatest time in which to live. More people have received the Holy Spirit in our day than at any other time in history. God is sending revival to everyone who will believe. If we do not live for God now, it is not likely that we would have lived for God in Christ's day or Paul's day. If we rebel against authority, it is likely that we would do so in another church or under another pastor. If we reject God's Word and ministry for our day, we would not be persuaded otherwise even if someone came back from the dead (Luke 16:29-31).

13. *Don't rely excessively on people, but look to the Lord for strength.* "Confidence in an unfaithful man in time of trouble is like a broken tooth, and a foot out of joint" (Proverbs 25:19). Just when you need that tooth or foot most, it will give way. It will cause severe pain when you least expect it. Therefore, in time of trouble, go to the Lord. Sometimes even your best friends will let you down. Sometimes the person you have confided in will tell others. Rather than discussing your problems with everyone, take them to the Lord.

14. *Control your spirit and your temper.* "He that hath no rule over his own spirit is like a city that is broken down, and without walls" (Proverbs 25:28). In ancient times, a city without walls was a city without protection. Likewise, a person without self-control is a person who has no protection for his or her spirit. Don't let your spirit get out of control. You have power to cast down imaginations and to control your thoughts (II Corinthians 10:5). If you excuse misconduct by saying, "That is my personality," then you are really saying, "I am not letting Christ have control of my personality." In this case, your wall of protection has fallen.

15. *Guard your integrity and reputation.* "A good name is rather to be chosen than great riches" (Proverbs 22:1). Your integrity is your most precious possession. Your reputation is important personally and also because you are part of the family of God. You have received the family name of Jesus, and everything you do reflects on that name.

When people hear your name, what do they think? Do they associate your name with hypocrisy, rebellion, pride, talebearing, dishonesty, or worldliness? Or do they think of sincerity, hard work, honesty, integrity, and spirituality? If the former, you will become a stumbling block to both believers and unbelievers. Keep your name and the name of your Lord above reproach.

16. *Be humble.* "Humble yourselves therefore under the mighty hand of God, that he may exalt you in due time" (I Peter 5:5-6). Humility is something you must acquire with intention and effort. Humility does not promote self. It does not act, look, or feel superior to others, including sinners. It does not pull someone else down in

order to go higher. It does not criticize others in order to get ahead of them. If God has given you a gift, use it to the glory of God, and let God open the right doors for you. You are in a spiritual race, but in this race everyone who reaches the finish line will receive a prize from God. You don't need to trip up someone else in order to win; everyone can be a winner.

17. *Guard against the things God hates.* In Proverbs 6:16-19, God took the time to list seven things that He especially hates. Take the time to ponder this list: "These six things doth the LORD hate: yea, seven are an abomination unto him: a proud look, a lying tongue, and hands that shed innocent blood, an heart that deviseth wicked imaginations, feet that be swift in running to mischief, a false witness that speaketh lies, and he that soweth discord among brethren." The abominable will not enter heaven (Revelation 21:8, 27). Therefore, if you are guilty in one of these areas, repent!

18. *Have your own convictions, and be true to them.* "Let every man be fully persuaded in his own mind" (Romans 14:5). Have a teachable spirit and accept by faith the Word of God and the voice of experience. At the same time, read the Bible and learn these things for yourself. "Prove all things; hold fast that which is good" (I Thessalonians 5:21).

Saints, do not force holiness teachings on others. Instead, pray for them and be good examples for them. Pastors, use wisdom with people, especially visitors and new converts. Realize that people who do not have the Holy Spirit cannot understand many things, and even if they understand they do not have power to obey fully. Realize that converts need time to develop personal convictions and an understanding of holiness principles. Do not force them to grow faster than they are able. Lead them, but make certain they understand each step of the way. Do not legislate holiness, but preach and teach the Word with wisdom and in a spiritual atmosphere so that God has the opportunity to change them.

In our day, many converts have come from such a sinful, ungodly background that it takes time and patience to bring them to Christian maturity. Our goal is to help them understand principles of holiness so that they will learn to think spiritually, read the Bible, pray, and develop their own convictions. Ultimately, if their hearts are not changed by the Spirit of God and if they do not understand the reasons for certain teachings, they will not follow them. It is better to give them time to develop personal beliefs than to confront them immediately with convictions that we have received through maturity. We must rely on the Word of God, the Spirit of God, and the example of the church to lead them into holiness of life.

19. *Love God and hate evil.* "The fear of the LORD is to hate evil" (Proverbs 8:13). You cannot be neutral; you either live for God, or you live contrary to His will. Love for God and hatred of evil are the most powerful defenses against Satan. All his devices are useless when you love God and hate evil. Evil talk, actions, and appearances will all vanish when you hate evil itself.

20. *Strive to be like Christ.* A Christian is literally someone who is Christ-like. When faced with a decision, ask yourself, "What would Jesus do?" Do not merely ask if there is a rule or regulation about something, but ask, "Would Jesus take pleasure in this activity? Would He be comfortable in this situation? Would He be pleased with

this decision?"

Holiness means imitating Jesus Christ. We must let Him have control of our personality and our mind. (See I Corinthians 2:16; Philippians 2:5.)

We can and must be holy because God is holy (I Peter 1:16). We will be holy if we let "Christ be formed" in us (Galatians 4:19). "Put on the new man, which after God is created in righteousness and true holiness" (Ephesians 4:24). By "perfecting holiness in the fear of God," we can "stand perfect and complete in all the will of God" (Colossians 4:12). Collectively, we can grow into "a perfect man, unto the measure of the stature of the fulness of Christ" (Ephesians 4:13).

Let us accept the challenge to search after and perfect holiness in our lives. May we truly be Christians—people who believe, love, obey, and become like our Lord and Savior Jesus Christ.

SCRIPTURE INDEX

SUBJECT INDEX

Works by David K. Bernard:

Pentecostal Theology Series
Vol. 1: The Oneness of God*
Vol. 2: The New Birth*
Vol. 3: In Search of Holiness (with Loretta Bernard)*
Vol. 4: Practical Holiness
A Study Guide for The Oneness of God
A Study Guide for The New Birth
A Study Guide for In Search of Holiness
A Study Guide for Practical Holiness
(Each volume can be purchased in hardback with Study Guide included)

Biblical Theology (Other)
A Handbook of Basic Doctrines*
Doctrines of the Bible (ed. with J. L. Hall)
In the Name of Jesus
Justification and the Holy Spirit
On Being Pentecostal (with Robin Johnston)
The Oneness View of Jesus Christ
Spiritual Gifts*
God's Infallible Word
Understanding God's Word

Practical Theology
The Apostolic Church in the Twenty-first Century
The Apostolic Life
Growing a Church
The Pentecostal Minister (ed. with J. L. Hall)
Spiritual Leadership in the Twenty-first Century

Commentaries
The Message of Colossians and Philemon
The Message of Romans

Booklets
Essential Doctrines of the Bible*
Essentials of Oneness Theology
Essentials of the New Birth*
Essentials of Holiness
Understanding the Articles of Faith
Bible Doctrines and Study Guide

Church History
A History of Christian Doctrine, Vol. 1: The Post-Apostolic Age to the Middle Ages
A History of Christian Doctrine, Vol. 2: The Reformation to the Holiness Movement
A History of Christian Doctrine, Vol. 3: The Twentieth Century
Oneness and Trinity, AD 100-300
The Trinitarian Controversy in the Fourth Century

CD
Pentecostal Digital Library, Vol. 1: Complete Works by David K. Bernard
Preaching the Apostolic Faith
Teaching the Apostolic Faith
Pentecostal Pulpit Series, Vol. 3: David K. Bernard (with audiovisual CD)
An Introduction to Apostolic Pentecostal Theology (4 books)

*Available in Spanish